The Day the Sky Fell

A family forever changed by MH17

MATTHEW HORDER

To my children, Sophie and Joshua

You were so young when your world changed. Losing your grandparents so suddenly and tragically is something no child should have to face. On top of that, you had to watch your dad navigate a grief that sometimes made him distant or distracted. Thank you for your patience, your resilience and for growing into such kind, genuine and thoughtful young people. I love you deeply. Keep looking out for each other and for your mum.

To Holly

Your unwavering support means more than I can ever fully express. You found a way to hold things together when everything felt like it was falling apart. You lost part of me that day, but you kept life ticking over for all of us, right down to the washing, without ever asking for thanks. I know this tragedy affected you too, in ways that often went unspoken. But you stayed, even when you didn't have to. You (almost) never complained. You just loved us through it. Thank you, from the deepest part of my heart.

To Susan and Howard

Two extraordinary people. Devoted parents. Adored grandparents. Their lives were taken in circumstances that no one should ever endure. Their love, wisdom and laughter remain with us always. I see you live on through my actions and behaviours every day. Thank you for giving me a great start in life. Forever remembered. Forever missed. Forever loved.

Contents

Foreword

On July 17, 2014, the world was confronted by an unimaginable tragedy when a commercial flight Malaysia Airlines MH17 was downed over eastern Ukraine. All 298 passengers and crew on board were killed, among them 38 Australians including families returning from holidays, loved ones coming home, others heading to work or to reunions. Their journeys were cut short in an act of unspeakable violence. From painstaking investigations over many years, we now know MH17 was shot down by a Russian Buk missile recklessly deployed into the conflict zone in Eastern Ukraine.

As Australia's Foreign Minister at the time, I played a leading role in our nation's response. From the moment the news broke, my focus was unwavering in seeking to secure access to the crash site, to repatriate with dignity the remains of the victims and to pursue a thorough, independent investigation that would deliver truth and accountability and hopefully closure for the grieving families and friends.

During my travels to the United Nations Security Council in New York, Ukraine, the Netherlands and beyond, I sought to contact every family of those 38 Australians and assure them of the Australian Government's absolute commitment to recovering the bodies, bringing them home and seeking justice. Supporting the bereaved families through those darkest days remains among the most emotional experiences of my life. I was inspired by their quiet strength and motivated by their profound grief and determination to honour the memory of those they lost.

The logistics of our national response were significant. Australia had no Embassy in Ukraine and our dedicated team of diplomats and experts, led by the Department of Foreign Affairs and Trade and Special Envoy Sir Angus Houston, were able to quickly establish a temporary office in a Kyiv hotel. We spent many hours in that location working through the vast complexities of gaining access to the crash site in a conflict region under the control of Russian-backed insurgents.

Australia worked closely with the government of the Netherlands to achieve the landmark United Nations Security Council Resolution 2166 in record time, adopted on July 21, 2014. The Resolution was instrumental in providing a legal basis for investigators to access the crash site and begin the long process of revealing how the tragedy occurred.

Working closely with my Netherlands counterpart, the indefatigable then Foreign Minister Frans Timmermans, we worked with the Ukraine leadership under President Petro Poroshenko to achieve reforms of Ukrainian law so that foreign investigation teams could deploy under their jurisdiction. This required an unprecedented recall of the Ukraine Parliament during the summer break to achieve a resounding majority in support of our efforts.

Matthew Horder's memoir, *The day the sky fell*, is a deeply moving and courageous account of one family's devastation in the wake of this global atrocity. Matthew's parents were among those lost that day and he chronicles the raw pain of sudden, violent bereavement and the long, often isolating, journey through grief. He weaves personal reflection with the broader quest for justice, including the meticulous work of the Joint

Investigation Team, the reconstruction of the aircraft as evidence and the human effort behind the search for answers amid political denial and disinformation, from Russia in particular.

What strikes me most about this book is its raw honesty. Grief is portrayed not as something to be overcome quickly, but as a lifelong companion that reshapes identity and purpose. Matthew's access to the investigative process offers key insights into the dedication of the investigators, police and forensic experts who laboured tirelessly to turn wreckage into testimony. Their work honoured the victims and gave voice to the families' demand that truth prevail.

In a world where disinformation erodes accountability, remembering MH17 is an important commitment to preventing a recurrence of the circumstances that lead to this tragedy. This memoir is more than a personal story. It is a testament to resilience, to the enduring power of love in the face of loss and to the importance of pursuing justice, no matter how protracted or challenging.

It is my hope that some comfort can be found from Matthew sharing his story with grace and clarity, for families who continue to carry this burden. His book *The day the sky fell* ensures that the lives cut short on that fateful day are never forgotten and that their legacy endures through the memories of those who will forever grieve their loss.

Hon Julie Bishop
Australia's Minister for Foreign Affairs
from 2013 until 2018

Preface

Driving into Gilze-Rijen Military Air Base in the south of the Netherlands, I knew that I was about to face possibly the most important piece of evidence in my lifetime. I had seen the photos and had a sense of what to expect, but nothing can prepare you for the real thing. As the bus turned a bend, there it was, the huge hangar. Looming ahead, waiting for our arrival.

I hopped off the bus and walked inside. It was vast, cold and silent. The kind of silence that carries weight, the kind that presses against your chest. And in the middle of it all stood what was left of MH17.

The front section of the aircraft had been painstakingly reconstructed – twisted metal, scorched panels, fragments of what once carried two hundred and ninety-eight lives through the sky. It was both familiar and foreign, the outline of a plane that once represented connection, movement, return, now a haunting skeleton of loss.

As I stepped closer, my eyes searched for where they had sat. Row numbers, window positions, things I once associated with boarding passes and holiday excitement, became coordinates of heartbreak.

Forever haunting, the reconstructed wreckage

There were no rows and there were no seats, just a shell of the plane. To stand where my parents had been sitting was almost unbearable. The air felt thick with absence. I could trace the line of the fuselage and imagine them there. Wondering what they were doing, talking about, maybe they were sleeping, the ordinary moments that ended in unimaginable violence.

The smell of metal and dust clung to everything. Perhaps it was the smell of death. I reached out but stopped short of touching it, as if doing so would break something fragile, disturb something sacred.

Around me, other family members and officials moved quietly. This wasn't just debris; it was a tomb, a testimony. Every fragment carried a name, a face, a story violently interrupted.

Standing there, I felt time collapse. The distance between that sky over Ukraine and this hangar in the Netherlands disappeared. I wasn't just looking at wreckage; I was standing inside loss itself. In that moment, I felt a post-traumatic stress response, but also a sense of healing.

And yet, among the destruction, there was also something else. Determination. Dignity. The sheer will of people who refused to let the truth stay buried. The fragments had been brought home to speak for those who no longer could. I couldn't help but marvel at the work done to collect the parts from the crash site and put them back together. It was fascinating yet so devastating.

I walked out of the hangar in silence. My legs were heavy, my heart even heavier. I carried something new with me: not just the pain of what was lost, but the certainty of what must never be forgotten.

I'm not sure why, but I wanted a photo. I grabbed my lawyer, who was with me, and asked her to take a photo. Just me and the plane. It's a haunting image; a moment in time that I will never forget.

How can something so brutal, so shocking, come from something so normal? My parents had boarded that plane after enjoying a fun-filled overseas trip. For several weeks, they had been visiting the United Kingdom, spending time with my brother in London, before finishing their trip in the Netherlands. Photos of the many highlights had filled their Facebook pages, and it was clear that the Netherlands was a special place and one that had brought them so much enjoyment. But it was from here that their lives were brought to this traumatic and sudden end. It was the final holiday that was never anticipated.

On July 17, 2014, Malaysia Airlines Flight MH17 was shot down over Eastern Ukraine. All two hundred and ninety-eight passengers and crew on board were killed, including thirty-eight Australians. My parents, Howard and Susan Horder, were among them. They were aged sixty-three and sixty-two.

The aircraft came down near the village of Hrabove in the Donetsk region, a place already fractured by war. Fields that once carried wheat and sunflowers were scarred by trenches and gunfire, claimed and reclaimed by Ukrainian soldiers and separatist fighters. By the European summer of 2014, the conflict had moved to the skies. Ukrainian military planes had been brought down – perhaps a warning in the clouds. Ukraine had closed its airspace below 32,000 feet, but commercial flights like MH17 were still permitted to fly above that altitude.

When MH17 disappeared from the radar at 1.20pm GMT, suspicion turned almost instantly to the separatists controlling the territory. Yet nothing about this conflict was simple. Behind the fighters stood another shadow: the hand of Russia, supplying weapons, intelligence and cover, while publicly denying they had any part in the devastation. At the time, the world was forced to speak in half-truths: Ukraine and separatists, a 'local' war, a disputed frontier. Russia's involvement was whispered, suspected, argued over, but not yet proven.

In the years that followed, the truth would come out. But in that first moment – on that fateful day in July 2014 – all that existed was wreckage scattered across a battlefield. And families left waiting for answers.

Right from day one, early reports suggested that the plane was brought down by a Russian missile system, which was later confirmed through legal proceedings. It was a devastating act that ended the lives of so many innocent people. My parents were simply heading home from what had been a wonderful holiday. It was something they had done many times before. They were minding their own business and blissfully unaware of the dangers of flying high above a region in turmoil. Their lives were taken so suddenly, so unfairly, and our lives were forever changed.

When a tragedy like this happens, people often say there are no words. But over time, you learn that there are words, sometimes hard to find, sometimes hard to say, but they're there. And this book is my attempt to give them shape.

This is my story. It's my perspective and my experience. Others may remember things differently, and that's okay. I don't expect everyone to agree with every detail; this is simply how I saw, felt and lived the tragedy.

For a long time, I struggled to explain what I've been through. There's been so much in my head – grief, anger, confusion, resilience. It often felt like too much to untangle. I used to say, 'I should put this all in a book', even though writing has never come easily to me. Writing is not something I've found enjoyable; it's always felt more like a chore. But this, finally, is me having a go. Getting these thoughts on paper is a deeply personal achievement and a mountain climbed. And, I can now say, writing this book has been a lot more satisfying than I ever imagined. Please note that in some cases, names may have been changed or intentionally omitted to protect people's privacy.

More than anything, I hope that sharing my lived experience will bring a sense of peace, for me, for my family and maybe even for someone else who's struggling. If these words help even one person, or shift the way something is done, then it's all been worth it.

The first day

When someone asks me what happened to my parents, I will often say they passed away suddenly. If I feel comfortable, I will say, "They were on board flight MH17, the plane that was shot down over Eastern Ukraine". The reality is, they were murdered. They were brutally murdered when the plane they were travelling in was deliberately blown out of the sky by a surface-to-air missile, tearing apart a commercial airliner mid-flight and scattering the bodies of two hundred and ninety-eight civilians, men, women and children across a war-torn field. Victims of a war they had nothing to do with. The crash site, located in a war zone, has since been described as the world's largest crime scene, over fifty square kilometres of wreckage and dead bodies. To put that into perspective, it is an area equivalent to around seven thousand rugby league fields.

I couldn't say goodbye. I was left watching from thousands of kilometres away. I immediately feel helpless. A helplessness that doesn't go away. It lingers like a silence you can't fill. It's the sort of thing you read about that happens to other people; it never happens to you. It was the biggest news story for days, weeks, possibly months and years, but in my life, it has been the biggest news story of a lifetime. Nothing can prepare you for what happened. Living it also does not prepare you to respond to or deal with it.

It sounds almost impossible, but my parents were murdered by Russian-backed separatists in Eastern Ukraine. And yet, as impossible or unrealistic as it sounds, it's true.

It was the morning of July 18, 2014. I was at home on Queensland's Sunshine Coast when I woke at around six. It was a typical winter morning. Except that when I checked my phone, I discovered multiple missed calls from both of my brothers, David and Adam. I had my phone on silent, my usual practice to get undisturbed sleep, so I had not heard the calls come through in the early hours of the morning. David was living in London at the time, so I could have excused a time-zone mix-up for the weird time he chose to call me. But Adam? He was only in Melbourne.

Something isn't right.

I got out of bed, careful not to wake my wife, Holly, and our children, Sophie and Joshua, who were sleeping soundly in their rooms. I felt an unexplained sense of urgency to address the missed calls. After a quick calculation of the time difference between London and Melbourne, I decided the best option was to phone Adam. He answered and had trouble speaking.

'Is everything okay?' My heart was pounding.

'I, I, I think… Mum and Dad's plane has crashed.'

'What are you talking about?'

This is ridiculous. He's being ridiculous. This makes no sense at all.

My head was spinning as Adam gathered himself to talk. I could immediately hear in his voice that he wasn't joking; he was tired and had been dealing with the enormity of it for hours. He somehow managed to tell me to turn the television on.

This can't be right.

I don't remember picking up the remote in the living room, but it was in my hand, and I turned it on. Channel 7 was running the *Sunrise* morning program.

The plane crash appeared to be the only story running that morning. The vision on the screen was of a burnt-out wreckage of a plane. The early footage was limited, but horrific and very dramatic. They played it on a loop with the caption along the bottom of the screen had words to the effect of – 'Malaysia Airlines flight crashed – no survivors'.

I knew Mum and Dad were travelling on Malaysia Airlines and I knew they were due back that day. I just watched the TV, immediately wanting more information, but at that point, there was nothing.

Adam stayed on the other end of the line. He was certain it was Mum and Dad's flight, but he wanted me to check the itinerary that Dad had left me. I grabbed my laptop and searched through emails with an urgency I had never experienced before.

My heart raced as I found the email, but fell out of my chest when I saw the flight number – MH17. The date matched: July 17, 2014.

'That's Mum and Dad's flight.'

I didn't know what to say; everything was a blur. 'I'll call you back,' I rushed out as I hung up the phone.

Maybe it isn't their flight.

I called Dad's mobile number, hoping he would answer, but I only got his recorded voice message.

By this time, Holly had woken up. She came out to the living room where I had the TV on. From the look on her face, she knew instantly something was wrong. When you've been married for nearly eleven years, you get a sense of what your partner is thinking.

'Is everything okay?' she kept her voice low so as not to wake the children.

My voice trembled, I had a lump in my throat and could barely speak. 'I think Mum and Dads plane has crashed.'

The fleeting looks on Holly's face reflected the way I felt when Adam first uttered those words to me – *you can't be serious?*

But her disbelief didn't last long; she could tell from my manner and disposition that I was serious, and the pictures on the TV provided some immediate confirmation. There wasn't much said at the time, but she gave me a hug. I turned the TV off.

I don't know why, but I asked her to sort the kids and take them to school. I didn't have the mental capacity to process what was happening, let alone pretend everything was okay. At least if the kids were at school, I could give myself a chance to work through the next steps. I had no idea where to start. I think I mentioned taking the day off and suggested that Holly do the same.

Holly leapt into action, getting the kids ready for the morning. I grabbed my laptop again to find some contact details to call the Department of Foreign Affairs and Trade (DFAT). I'd seen on the TV that there was a number that was available, the Consular Emergency Centre hotline. I'd never called DFAT before – I'd never been in that position before.

I spent an hour or so on the phone waiting to speak to someone. I couldn't understand why I couldn't get through. *Why is everyone calling the hotline? Surely it is only for families impacted?* It seemed there was no easy way to get through, but I held my position in the queue.

The longer wait just made things worse. It gave my brain all the space it needed to create horrible thoughts of all the possibilities running through my head, competing for space. My anxiety level was through the roof. I think I knew deep down what my parents' fate was, but I wanted to know for sure.

After checking Mum and Dad's itinerary for a second and third time, I knew it was their flight. I knew Mum and Dad were meticulous with their travel plans. We had missed a flight from Hawaii to Australia in 1987 and

*Howard and Susan in Maastricht for André Rieu
just six days before they were killed*

the family was stuck in Honolulu for three days. They had never missed a flight since. They would have been at the airport early, ready for that boarding call.

Is it possible they got it wrong again? I doubted it, but I was hoping above all else that someone would tell me it wasn't true. While I was waiting, I started working through Dad's dossier he had left me. He always sent me something before they went away. It was very detailed and a great lesson for everyone in being prepared for a sudden loss.

He had sent it to me on June 12, eight days before they flew out to Heathrow in London. The first line read: 'In the unlikely event that something might happen to both of us while we are away, you will need some information...' It then detailed sixteen points, including some personal details and valuable contact numbers and names I would use. Mum and Dad's doctor, solicitor, insurance policy numbers for health, cars and house, Medicare numbers, bank account details, credit card numbers and superannuation accounts all meticulously laid out for me. The level of information was useful.

I eventually got through to consular assistance, but they couldn't really tell me anything. I realise now that they were being cautious. The lady on the other end of the phone was very professional. She's had a tough morning; I could tell in her voice that there was a whole new level of stress that you could only have on a day like today.

They obviously knew of the crash but didn't have confirmation of the flight manifest. She asked me lots of questions, and I was able to respond to almost everything thanks to Dad's dossier. The one thing I couldn't provide was passport numbers. I didn't have a copy, and the details weren't in Dad's dossier. Not having the passport details was troubling me; I felt I should have them, especially at that moment when I was trying to confirm something so serious. Perhaps it could have confirmed something sooner. She took all my details and said someone would call me back.

The moments after that phone call were a bit surreal. By then, the kids had finished breakfast and were ready for school. I said goodbye to them and Holly took them to school. For Sophie and Joshua, it was as if nothing had happened; perhaps they were wondering why Dad hadn't gone to work. I wanted to tell them, but it was not the right time. I wanted to keep them home, but school was the best place for them. I'm sure they knew something was up, but I kept telling myself that routine was the best thing. This would prove true in the coming months.

They had left and I was in the house on my own. The noise of the morning had gone and it felt incredibly silent. The distractions of the TV, DFAT and kids getting ready for the day were gone. I could feel myself and my senses for the first time. I noticed a lump in my throat and tension in my forehead, neck and shoulders. I was getting a headache that ended up lasting for months. It's a headache that still returns regularly. I remember searching the internet for any news; it was the lead story for what seemed like every outlet. Early reporting suggested that the plane had been shot down. *How do they know*, I thought to myself.

I forced myself to eat breakfast, so I had a bowl of cereal. I didn't feel like eating, but I knew I had to, despite the lump in my throat making it an extremely difficult task. On reflection, I see I had this subconscious sense that I needed to look after myself. There were moments when this protection mechanism kicked in, and even though something as simple as eating is a basic need, I could see how easy it could be to spiral out of control if I didn't look after myself.

After breakfast, I telephoned both my brothers, first Adam and then David. I was able to relay my discussion with DFAT and the consular emergency centre.

This was my first chance to speak with David, and it became clear he was the first of the three of us to find out about the plane going down. He had received one of those news notifications on his phone and pieced it together. Mum and Dad had spent some time with David in London during their travels.

Prior to boarding their flight, he received a text message from our parents wishing him well and looking forward to seeing him at Adam's wedding later that year. Adam and I didn't speak for long, but it was enough to understand what he had been through over the last several hours. It was horrible for him as it had been for David. I wish we could have been closer in that moment.

Because we were so spread out, it was difficult to know what to do. We discussed various options. As the eldest at 39, I immediately felt a sense of responsibility and subconsciously assumed the role of coordinating the family. We briefly discussed travelling to Ukraine to try and help but quickly decided that was not a great option. I considered the best course was for my brothers to join me in Queensland, as this was the location of our parents' home, and being together seemed more important than anything else at that stage. Both Adam and David made the necessary arrangements to get to Queensland.

Adam and his fiancé arrived the next day, while David was incredibly brave and hopped on a flight to come back to Australia from London. I don't know how he did it. He arrived in the early hours of Sunday, July 20.

Amid all the early phone calls that morning, I somehow managed to ring my manager at work, Steve. It must have been one of the strangest calls he's ever received from a team member asking for a day off. I remember saying something like, 'I can't come in today. It looks like my parents were on board the plane that crashed in Ukraine.' Just like that.

I often wonder what it was like for Steve to hear those words and how the office responded that day. These things impact everything. I didn't go to work that day, and I didn't return for three months. In fact, I didn't think about work once during that time, such was the enormity and circumstances of the loss.

Not having copies of Mum and Dad's passports was playing on my mind; I wanted to find those details. *I'm sure there will be a copy in their house.* Holly was finished dropping the kids off at school, so we got ready, jumped in the car and drove to Brisbane.

It's a throwaway line, but that day became probably the worst and hardest day of my life. When I reflect on what we did, I still don't know how we even functioned, and it puts many other aspects of life into perspective. What used to seem urgent, stressful or important at work or in everyday life suddenly fades into the background. I found myself questioning things I'd once taken for granted. Deadlines didn't matter. Petty disagreements didn't matter.

What did matter was people. My family. My kids. Holly. Friends who checked in. Strangers who showed kindness. The raw fragility of life became clear. You learn just how quickly everything can change, and with that comes a deeper appreciation for the moments we usually rush through. It doesn't mean you stop caring about the rest of life, but you carry this new lens with you. A recalibration of sorts. You start measuring things differently.

Perspective isn't something that just clicks into place, though. It's something I've had to keep coming back to, especially on the hard days. But once you've lived through this kind of loss, you can't unsee the value of what truly matters.

The hardest words

Mum and Dad's home was in Albany Creek on the outskirts of Brisbane. Given that it was only about an hour's drive from our place on the Sunshine Coast, I was fortunate to have visited and spent time there regularly. However, I never had a key to the property, and to be honest, I never really needed it. Despite this, I knew I could get into Mum and Dad's house. I had Dad's dossier with me, which included detailed instructions on finding the hidden key and getting into the house.

> 'There is a spare set of keys hidden under a small rock in the rock wall at the back, just up and along from the hose. They will open the front screen door and the front door. As soon as you enter, you will need to open the security system panel and punch in the code to disarm the security.'

In the end, I felt like I was breaking in. My anxiety levels were high. To get to the backyard of the house, I needed to climb a six-foot fence, since the side gates had locks, then climb it again to get back to the front door. But with Dad's dossier, I felt like he was talking to me. Mission accomplished; I got through the front door, disarmed the alarm and was in the house.

One of the first things I noticed was how perfect the house was. Mum and Dad were always neat and tidy and had everything in order, but this place looked like it was ready to be put on the market. The real estate photographer could come straight in and take all the photos; there was nothing to do. We kept it that way for a long time. My mission at that stage was clear – I needed to get my hands on whatever documentation we needed.

Holly and I began looking for a copy of their passports, a photocopy or a record of the passport numbers would have sufficed. The focus area was mainly around the office. It seemed like we searched for hours, and there was a sense of panic as the search kept coming up blank. I felt helpless in that moment; it was supposed to help DFAT with their search for Mum and Dad. I never found a record of the passport details. I felt terrible, but if Dad had left a copy, they would have turned up.

I checked over the house once more, but there was nothing to take care of at that moment. I locked the house and returned the key under the small rock. Exactly the way I found it. I probably could have just kept it, but I wasn't ready for that yet. We hopped in the car and headed over to Mum's parents' place in Chermside, not far from Albany Creek.

One of the interesting things about Grandma and Grandpa's place is that they moved into the house on their wedding day and lived there together for the rest of their married life, some sixty-seven years, well into their nineties. A second interesting fact is that Dad's childhood house was a few doors down and was built by the same builder, with the same original layout as Mum's.

When we arrived, both Grandma and Grandpa were crying. Even though I hadn't spoken to them yet, they had spoken with both of my brothers. They had the TV on, which was playing endless footage of the crash. And the broadcast seemingly confirmed that this was a deliberate act and that the plane was shot down. It really wasn't helpful. How could Grandma and Grandpa even comprehend this? The initial arrival at the house was a little chaotic. I think they were hoping I had some different news or an update. Of course I didn't.

I remember taking Grandpa aside and trying to talk with him. He was a pragmatic man who was often very logical and could make reason of just about anything. He saw through you if something was silly or stupid and didn't waste too much time on things that weren't worth worrying about. But that day was different. He was a broken man. I don't think I've ever seen anyone sadder than Grandpa on that day.

He said words to the effect of 'I shouldn't have let them go.' The kind of words a father would say to try and protect his daughter and keep her safe. There was no way he could have predicted what happened, and no chance he could have prevented it. It didn't feel like real life; it was more like something you might watch in a movie.

This was the only time I had seen Grandpa cry. Grandpa didn't say much, but I knew he was feeling like he could have stopped them. His heart was broken. This isn't how it is supposed to be. At their age, you expect to be able to outlive your children.

Grandma kept saying, 'I told Susan not to do it…' It was something she would say daily for many years to come. Again, a mother just trying to protect her daughter, but to no avail.

At the time, Grandma was suffering from the early stages of dementia. This was probably where it was the hardest for her. It was as if every time she saw the news or heard about Mum and Dad, it was the first time all over again. Time and time again, Grandma was reliving the news. And time and time again, she stated she told them not to do it. It was hard to watch and live through. Grandma was stuck in those early stages of grief where denial is your initial reaction. All we could do was support her through it all.

The day seem to move quickly and the time came to get home and pick the kids up from school. Without a doubt, the most difficult job of the day was ahead of me – I needed to tell the kids what happened. During the drive home, I tried to think of the best way to communicate something so devastating. *Do I just play it down? Let them know that their grandparents passed away?* The truth seemed so much harder and confronting for young kids. I had no real plan, but decided honesty was the best approach.

As a father, you never want to do anything to upset your kids. Despite thinking about it for much of the drive home, I had no real plan or strategy. I had not had a chance to fully process the news myself. I had so many unanswered questions of my own. *How did this happen? Why did it happen? How do we carry on? What happens next?* The loss was sudden, violent and public. I was drowning in disbelief and sorrow. But I also knew I had to tell my children before they found out elsewhere. Being so public, there was always a chance they would hear about it, and I needed them to know fact from fiction, despite not having the facts myself. I knew that the plane my parents were booked to travel on had gone down, and no one had survived. My gut told me that if I didn't say something, they would hear about it through their friends, in the playground at school, or from another family member. They might see their grandparents' faces on TV. Even though I knew very little myself, it had to happen now, with honesty, love and within the safety of our own home.

Sophie was seven and Josh was just five. My parents were known to them as Gran and Pa. I sat them down in the lounge, trying to calm my own emotions while knowing I was about to change their world forever. I tried to steady my voice while my heart felt like it was breaking into pieces. I didn't have perfect words – there are no perfect words for something like this – but I knew I had to be honest and present for them.

Holly was with me to support this process. It is difficult to know how I found the courage. I kept it simple but honest as I calmly explained, 'Gran and Pa's plane crashed, and they both died.'

I told them that no one had survived. There was no sugar coating it and no skirting the issue. Up front and honest. I had always felt that honesty was the best approach. They both burst into tears; their grief was immediate. That day, I shared the news that broke my two adorable children's hearts. They were fortunate to have a close and happy relationship with my parents, which made the news even harder to bear. This was news that would forever reshape them.

I decided early on that they should always have the truth about their grandparents so they could discern the misinformation put in front of them. And as it turned out, that was the best way, and I don't think I could have done it any differently. Sometimes, when you do things in the moment, without overthinking and trusting your gut, it seems to work out or be the best approach. Normality was also key for the kids. It was a Friday afternoon, and on the Monday, the kids went to school. Despite everything, routine was still the best thing for the kids, and ultimately, I think it was the best thing for me.

In those moments, I learned that breaking terrible news to children doesn't require perfect words; it requires truth, gentleness and presence. I held them close; I didn't want to let go. I answered the questions I could and admitted the ones I couldn't. I tried not to hide my own sadness. I wanted them to know it was okay to grieve.

There is no guidebook for this kind of grief. No right way to break terrible news to children. Even now, there is a part of me stuck in the moment, knowing their world had changed forever. Perhaps I was realising that my world had changed forever, too. I just hadn't realised it at the time.

And from that moment on, we began the long, slow journey of making sense of a senseless loss, together. Although nothing could really prepare us for what was ahead.

The downing of a commercial flight was always going to be big news, but for Malaysia Airlines, this meant they had lost a second flight within a matter of months. Early that same year, on March 8, flight MH370 disappeared, and at the time of writing, it had never been found. The comparison between the two was immediate, even though they were different in circumstance. To this day, I still must explain the difference between the two flights. Often, when someone hears about my parents' fate, they exclaim that it must be hard not knowing what happened to them.

'Nope, we are the other one, we got our parents' bodies back, we've had a funeral,' I would say.

The news spread quickly, and the media outlets were eager for the next headline. Receiving official information on that first day was difficult, so the media had started contacting families. I started receiving a great many calls on both the home phone and my mobile. Over the course of the day and into the evening, I received countless calls, most of them from journalists, but there were some calls from family and friends. It felt like representatives of every television and radio news program and every newspaper in Australia contacted us. There were also calls from overseas media – think CNN, BBC and the like. The media interest was immediate, and it was intense.

The grief hadn't even sunk in before the media arrived. The headlines were written before I even had time to process a single word. Mum and Dad were gone, and already the world wanted quotes, photos and tears. The media didn't want to tell our story; they just took it from us.

The calls were relentless. Most of the time, the media were just guessing. They were searching for my parents, most likely on social media and connecting me as a son. They would call so confidently and ask to speak with me about my parents. Holly would receive the phone calls, too.

'Hello, it's such-and-such from [insert media organisation], can I talk to you about your parents?' This is how I knew they were guessing.

They had an attitude of doing whatever it took to get a fresh take on this event. Never considering that we were experiencing the worst days of our lives. That didn't matter; they were just doing their job. They kept calling, as if I owed them something, as if our personal tragedy were a public asset.

I remember opening the front door a day or two after the downing, thinking it might be someone bringing us food or checking in; instead, it was a stranger with a camera and a reporter asking how I felt. I didn't even know how to breathe.

I turned on the TV, the evening news was starting, and a picture of Mum and Dad was on the screen. My mum and dad's smiling faces on the TV. I couldn't believe it. *How did they get that? How did they know?* I turned the TV off.

I didn't fully appreciate it at the time, but it's easy to look back now and see that this was a global incident of epic proportions. Headlines screamed across every time zone: 'Flight MH17 Shot Down over Ukraine'. It was a civilian plane shot down over a war zone. Maps, missiles, experts, blame – it was dissected like a political event, not a plane full of real people.

The public was hooked and mostly outraged. This type of thing should never happen. Everyone seemed to have an opinion. Our family's heartbreak was part of the news cycle, sandwiched between footage of the wreckage and sound bites from world leaders. But for me, it wasn't about airspace violations or missile trajectories. It was Mum and Dad. It was about those two seats on that flight. Two lives. A part of my world ended that day as the rest of the world watched in horror. They were my parents, and no headline could ever hold that weight.

It was getting to the back end of a busy day, and I just remember feeling lost. *How do we know what to do? Where to from here?*

I then received a call from an officer at DFAT.

'We have just received a copy of the passenger manifest, and I'm sorry, but your parents' names are on it.'

The rest of the world already knew, but at least now, we knew officially.

The person on the other end of the line was clearly stressed, their voice was trembling, and you could hear the strain. 'Someone will be in touch tomorrow.'

We hung up. I wondered how many of those phone calls they had made that day. I still had more phone calls to make.

One of the missed calls I had during the day was from Kay Cherry, who was Mum's childhood friend with a relationship spanning more than five decades. In fact, Kay may have rung several times. I don't think I took the calls initially, as I wanted to give my mum's best friend more time on the phone when I called back.

My brothers and I had known Kay our whole lives; we had grown up having play dates and outings with Kay's family. It took me days to respond to some calls, but with Kay, it was different. While I didn't call Kay back immediately, it wasn't because I didn't want to; rather, I wanted more information myself. At least, now that I had the information from DFAT, I could chat with Kay.

It wasn't late, but it was getting late to be making phone calls. Nonetheless, I phoned Kay. I did not have to say anything to her. As soon as she answered the phone, she cried. She knew. My heart sank.

'I'm sorry Kay. Mum was on the plane.'

Kay had lost her friend; I could feel the heartbreak through the earpiece. By the time I had spoken to Kay, it was all over the news. I felt bad for not speaking to her sooner, but there are no rules when it comes to this stuff.

We talked for a while; I can't really remember the details. I do remember feeling like I was supporting Kay through the initial shock. We might have been supporting each other. I remember asking if she had someone with her. Tracey, her eldest daughter, had been sitting with her during the call. At least I knew Kay was supported. We would chat further in the coming days and indeed over the next ten or so years.

During the day, I had also received some panicked calls from one of Dad's golfing friends, John Bosch. John knew that our parents were due to travel back that day and had been travelling on that airline. His messages were along the lines of, 'Just checking to confirm that the news is not true.'

Like it was some kind of mistake.

'Can you just call me back and tell me it is all good?'

Of course, he had been trying to call Dad that day and couldn't get through. There was only one reason he was phoning me, he knew. They had lost a friend and a golfing mate. So sad and just horrible for all of them to endure.

This was day one, ground zero if you like. My parents had died in a plane crash. We were learning that the plane crashed in what could only be described as a complex area, and that it was more than just a simple crash, but more likely a deliberate act. We had no idea how complex, and that realisation didn't sink in for weeks.

It was the end of a long day and time for bed. *How can I sleep?* I can't remember sleeping well, but I must have got something. I remember waking up, seeing the daylight the next day and thinking that the world was still spinning. While it hadn't ended, it felt like my world had.

Shaping life through love and lessons

Mum often had some sayings or words of wisdom. One of her favourites was, 'Don't sweat the small stuff.' And she was right.

She would say it to us kids just as much as she would to Dad. It was more than just a saying; it was how Mum would live her life, and I think that set the tone for my parents' relationship. It was something that set them on a path of one of the happiest and most supportive partnerships you could imagine.

They shared the kind of bond that seemed to grow stronger with time. It wasn't loud or showy, but steady and enduring, built on decades of shared values and the comfort of knowing someone inside out. They both came from good homes, which was the perfect foundation for their relationship. They met young, grew together and stood side by side through all of life's highs and lows. From building a home to raising a family, their love was the foundation that everything else rested on. They were a partnership in every sense of the word.

Even in the moments before their tragic death, they were still a team. They didn't just love each other; they liked each other, and they were friends. They made each other laugh, knew when to give space and showed affection in small but meaningful ways. Their connection was lived more than spoken, but it was unmistakable. In the end, they left this world as they had lived in it – together, with a love at the centre of it all that cannot be questioned.

Mum and Dad grew up just a few doors down from each other on Hilltop Avenue in Chermside, a northern Brisbane suburb. They lived in their identical houses – same builder, same 1930s highset Queensland design. In some ways, their lives began as mirror images, childhoods unfolding side by side, unaware of what the future would hold.

Dad was born on October 30, 1950, at Brisbane's Royal Women's Hospital to Norman and Ethel Horder and was named Howard Ramon Horder. We always joked that Dad's initials were HRH, His Royal Highness.

Mum, Susan Marilyn Black, arrived a year later, on October 9, 1951, to Rex and Joyce Black. October was always an exciting time as we had two birthdays to celebrate.

Hilltop Avenue was the kind of street where everyone's mum kept an eye on the neighbourhood. It was a post-war suburb full of Hills Hoists washing lines, Victa lawn mowers, modest gardens and the low hum of Brisbane summers. Mum and Dad went to the same schools, probably passed each other on the way to class or waved across front yards. But it wasn't until later, as teenagers, that their friendship began to turn into something more.

There's something poetic about that – two lives beginning just metres apart, destined to intertwine. They didn't grow up in wealth, but they grew up in stability. In ordinary houses made extraordinary by the lives that filled them. It set the tone for the kind of home they would later build together for my brothers and me – grounded, steady and full of unspoken love.

In 1969, before Mum and Dad had really started dating, Mum wrote Dad a letter. It is a handwritten letter posted from the Gold Coast's Coolangatta, where Mum was staying with Kay and her family. It was a beautiful letter that Dad had kept. The first we knew of the letter was when we found it sorting through Mum and Dad's things following their death.

Mum likely had no idea it would be kept. But Dad held onto that letter for the rest of his life. Tucked away folded and safe, it travelled with Dad through every chapter of their lives together. It wasn't just paper and ink; it was a marker of the beginning, a symbol of something meaningful even then. That Dad kept it says everything about how much she meant to him, even before they were officially together.

My parents married in 1972, when Mum was just twenty and Dad was twenty-one, beginning a life together with love, family and simple

Susan and Howard on their wedding day in 1972

ambitions. At the time, they were living in their first place, a modest home in west Chermside.

Just a year later, they purchased a block of land in Albany Creek for $7000, a price that seems almost unimaginable today. They paid a $2 holding deposit, a small but symbolic step towards building their future. Dad had kept a copy of the handwritten receipt as proof that the $2 holding deposit had been paid. Not long after, they began construction on a house that would become our family home for many years, a place filled with memories, milestones and the gentle rhythm of everyday life. It was more than a house; it was the foundation of everything to come.

Mum went to teaching college and taught at Stafford State School. She was a natural nurturer, and my brothers and I really benefited from that while growing up. Mum fell pregnant with me and stopped working. Dad took his role of provider seriously, working two or three jobs at a time so Mum could stay home and dedicate herself to raising the family. David was born in 1977, followed by Adam in 1981. We were all born in March, which is not surprising as our parents were so organised.

I would mostly describe my life before MH17 as 'normal', though I've never really liked that word. To me, normal assumes everyone's life looks and feels the same, when in reality, each of us lives through our own mix of challenges, joys and moments that shape us. I certainly had my share of significant events growing up, but at the time, they were simply part of life, things I dealt with without much reflection. It's only now, while writing this book, that I've come to see how each of those moments, big and small, played a part in shaping who I am. That life, with its familiar pattern, felt steady until July 17, 2014, when everything changed in an instant.

I was born in March 1975 at the same hospital my parents were born in – the Royal Women's. Mum and Dad were in the house they had built at Albany Creek and that is where I grew up and spent a large amount of my childhood. Albany Creek was a semi-rural suburb on the outskirts of

Brisbane. The area was transitioning from its agricultural roots to a more residential community, as there was always development occurring. It was a quieter lifestyle, with open spaces, and I would say a strong sense of community. There was a lot of bushland and farmland in the surrounding area – so many places for us to explore, get outside and play. Progressive development of infrastructure and housing gradually shaped Albany Creek into the suburb it is today, which is still full of families and very much a suburban area in greater Brisbane.

I grew up with what I now understand was privilege. Not the kind you see in mansions, luxury cars or private jets, but the kind that shows up in more enduring ways: two parents who loved me and took good care of me, a home that felt safe, and a world where school uniforms were always clean, and dinner was always on the table. We weren't rich, but we never went without. Eating out was a treat, something you did only on special occasions, like a birthday.

Mum and Dad worked tirelessly to give David, Adam and myself the best start in life. They poured their energy into creating a home that was safe, supportive and full of love. They sacrificed without complaint, showed up without fail and taught us the value of hard work, kindness and sticking together. Whether it was late nights, early mornings or the constant effort that goes unnoticed by the world, they did it all for us. Their love wasn't just something we felt; it was something they showed us every single day.

Dad worked hard, long hours, often quietly and always steadily, and in my early years, took on those additional jobs – mowing lawns and concreting – to help pay the bills. Mum made the house feel like the centre of something warm and solid. I had access to good schools, stable friendships and the kind of suburban freedom where you could disappear for hours and still be home in time for tea. At the time, I didn't know to call it privilege. It was just my life. But looking back, I see how much that foundation gave me and how much of who I am was shaped by it.

Albany Creek felt like a secret pocket on the edge of Brisbane. People often joked that it was in the middle of nowhere, before the roundabouts multiplied and the suburbs spilled over every hill. We played outside and rode bikes until the streetlights came on, made cubbies in the surrounding bushland, knew which creeks and waterways to catch tiny fish and shrimp, and where all the good bike jumps were.

Everyone seemed to know your name, or at least one of my siblings'. Being a Creeker wasn't something we ever said out loud back then, but it lived in the way we spoke, the shortcuts we knew, the bush tracks we used to explore. Our schools were new compared to others, and both the primary and high schools were within a short walking distance from home. I completed my primary years at Albany Hills State School, which was only a year old when I started pre-school.

I remember one day in Year One coming home from school, and Adam was there in one of those baby bouncers. It was my first memory of having the third child and another brother in the house. My primary school years were largely uneventful as far as school was concerned. I seemed to cruise through without much effort. I had good friend groups, some of whom I am still friends with today.

Life was eventful in other areas, though. In 1982, I underwent open-heart surgery to repair a congenital heart defect, a hole in the septum of my heart. The heart defect was diagnosed at birth, initially as a murmur, and monitored from an early age. From very early on, it was decided that I would need heart surgery; however, as was the practice at the time, the medical team preferred to wait until I was older to operate. So, I was seven before the surgery took place.

At that age, I didn't fully grasp the seriousness of it. I understood that something was wrong, something needed fixing, but I couldn't quite wrap my head around the fact that they would have to open my chest to do it. Open-heart surgery. The words alone seemed to belong to a different world, one where I was both present and strangely detached, like an observer of my own life.

The operation required my chest to be opened through a midline sternotomy; my breastbone was cut straight down the middle to give the surgeons access to my heart. I was placed on a heart-lung bypass machine while the team carefully closed the defect. It was a major operation for such a small body. I don't remember the surgery itself, but I remember the lead-up, the sterile smell of the hospital and the long days of recovery. I still carry the scar today, forty-three years later, right down the centre of my chest. A permanent reminder of what I went through, and what my parents carried with me.

The surgery took place at Prince Charles Hospital in Chermside. At the time, Prince Charles Hospital was one of the leading cardiac hospitals in the Southern Hemisphere and still performs many heart and lung surgeries today. The hospital was a world unto itself, with white walls, hushed voices, beeping monitors and that distinct smell of antiseptic that stays with you. I remember lying in that bed in the hours before surgery, staring up at the ceiling tiles and wondering what would happen when I woke up. *Will I wake up?* It's a question that flickers in the back of your mind, even when you're young and people are trying their best to keep your calm.

My parents were carrying a weight I couldn't yet comprehend. I've looked back on that time often, not just through the lens of my own experience, but through theirs. As a parent myself, I wonder how they even managed it. What must it have felt like for them to be told their child needed open-heart surgery? To try and look brave when all they probably wanted to do was fall apart? If they were falling apart, they certainly didn't show it. My parents gave me the calmness that I needed at such a young age.

My mum and dad sat next to me before they wheeled me away. I am sure they were trying not to cry. My brothers must have been with one of our grandparents. Mum would rub my hair like she always did, and I am sure it was calming. Dad hovered close by. He didn't say much, his eyes were set hard ahead, jaw clenched. He was holding it together for me. I don't think he took much time off work; I remember the stay in hospital where he would visit before work and again after work. It must have been so exhausting for him. I know now that the surgery was just as much theirs to endure as it was mine. Maybe more.

When they rolled me into the operating room, I don't remember being scared in the way adults are scared. I remember hating the hospital. I was sick of needles and tests, something to this day I still dislike. I remember everyone being great around me, the nurses, the doctors, the reassuring voice telling me to count backwards. Trust was a luxury I had as a child. My parents had no such insulation. They had to stand outside the doors and wait, hours that must have felt like days, not knowing, only hoping. That kind of waiting leaves a scar, too, even if you can't see it.

The surgery was a success. The hole in my heart was closed. I don't remember waking up, exactly, more like resurfacing slowly, through layers of pain and confusion. My chest hurt in a way I'd never felt before. Breathing was difficult, moving even harder. My first memory waking up was in intensive care. I just remember being unwell, the smell of sickness and that awful antiseptic smell. But I was alive, and every ache reminded me of that simple truth. After a couple of days, I moved to a ward. I had the option of being wheeled in my bed or in a wheelchair. I'd never been in a wheelchair before, and being seven I picked the wheelchair. The excitement wore off quickly, as by the time I got to the ward, I was exhausted and wanted to lie down; I should have selected the bed.

In the days that followed, I saw my parents differently. They were everywhere, helping me sit up, encouraging me to eat, helping me when

I took my first steps down the hall with the IV pole clattering beside me. I saw the exhaustion in their eyes, the weight they had carried. And even at that young age, I understood something important – they had been through the fire too. One of my clearest memories after the surgery was the plastic breathing device they gave me. It had three coloured balls inside clear tubes, and the goal was to make them rise by inhaling deeply through a mouthpiece. It was called an incentive spirometer, though I didn't know the name at the time; I just knew it was hard. Each breath pulled at the stitches in my chest and strained my lungs, but my parents and the nurses encouraged me gently, explaining that it was helping my lungs recover and keeping my chest clear. To a seven-year-old, it felt more like a strange little game, but it was serious work, and part of the long road to healing.

I have no doubt that that experience changed me. It shaped how I see the world, how I understand vulnerability, courage and love. The scar may have faded, but it never disappeared. And I wouldn't want it to. It's a part of me, a reminder of the day my life was put back together and of the two people who never let it fall apart.

Resilience isn't something you're handed. I believe it's something you grow into, often without realising it, and usually because life leaves you no other choice.

After the surgery, I thought the hard part was over. The danger had passed, the hole in my heart had been closed, and I was supposed to be 'fixed'. That's what people said: I looked better, sounded stronger and was on the road to recovery. But inside, something was still raw. I had faced death, even if I hadn't fully understood it at the time, and that experience left me changed in ways that weren't visible on an X-ray or hospital chart.

I remember how slow the healing was. Getting out of bed was a battle. Lifting my arms hurt. Laughing hurt. Even breathing felt like a test. I hated the weakness. I hated relying on others. I hated feeling like something fragile. But each day, I got up. Not out of heroism, but because I didn't know what else to do. I got up, and I tried to walk a little farther, breathe a little deeper. I don't ever remember crying, but maybe I did. I was a young kid, so I'm sure I had my moments especially when I had another needle.

Looking back, I think that's where resilience begins, not just with strength, but with some kind of stubbornness. The kind that doesn't make speeches but keeps showing up. I wasn't fearless. I was afraid most of the time. But I didn't let that fear tell me who I was going to be.

School eventually came back into the picture. So did routines, responsibilities and the awkwardness of being 'the kid who had heart surgery'. I felt different. Not just physically, but emotionally. I had seen a side of life most kids hadn't, and it set me slightly apart. It was like an invisible border surrounded me that no one else could see. I remember having to sit out of many physical activities. I wasn't allowed to exert myself for many months. If I got puffed, I had to stop. It would be another seven years before I was fully cleared for normal activity. But inside that border, I started to build something strong. My body had been repaired, but my identity was still under construction.

Resilience, I learned, is not just about pushing through pain. It's about accepting that pain has a place in the story. There's no going back to who you were before a major event. There's only forward. And that forward is rarely straight. It comes in starts and stumbles, in moments where you want to quit, and in moments where, despite everything, you don't.

My parents had their own kind of resilience. They didn't talk about what the surgery did to them, not really. But I saw it in how they carried on, how they watched over me and how they managed the numerous medical appointments following the surgery. More protective, maybe. But also, more grateful. We all were. The surgery gave us time we might not have had, and that realisation stays with you.

After the surgery, I continued to see a cardiologist for regular follow-up appointments. For seven years, those check-ups were part of my life, a slow, steady process of monitoring, testing and being reassured that my heart was healing as it should and growing with my body as I got older. Eventually, I was given the all-clear, and that chapter closed.

To this day, I don't always feel strong. But I know I am. Not because I never fell, but because I always got up. Sometimes shakily. Sometimes with help. Always with intention. That's resilience. It doesn't look like triumph; it looks like continuity. Like persistence. And somewhere along the way, you stop just surviving and start living again. Fully, deeply and with a heart, once broken, that beats with purpose. Looking back, I can see now how these experiences helped shape me for what was to come.

Life before MH17

I have always loved travel and loved flying. Ironically, I still do. It is a passion that started early, thanks to my parents' commitment to family holidays.

As kids, we took holidays every year. Many of these were caravanning with Mum and Dad – numerous beach trips north to the Sunshine Coast's Caloundra or south to Yamba on the New South Wales coastline. Dad would tow a 22-foot caravan, with all the gear, plus a tinny on the roof of the car and us three boys in the back seat. It was supposed to be a holiday, but it must have been exhausting. There were years when we would take an initial three-week holiday (or more) at the Hibiscus Caravan Park in Caloundra, usually in January just after Christmas and New Year, and then leave the caravan set up there, travelling back there every weekend until Easter. We would then have two weeks at the park over the Easter break before packing everything up and coming home. Great memories and experiences for my brothers and me.

In 1987, when I was twelve, we were fortunate to take our first overseas trip; in fact, it was the first time we had been on a plane, as all our trips before that had been by car. Mum and Dad had done a lot of travelling overseas for various work trips and conferences associated with Dad's work. And for this trip, there was an option to take children (which Mum and Dad had to pay for), and they decided to take us. The trip was to the United States of America and included stops in Los Angeles, San Francisco and Waikiki.

There is no doubt this trip gave me the love of travel that I have today. And why wouldn't it? LA was amazing because it had Hollywood, Disneyland and the Santa Monica Pier. Throw in cable cars in San Francisco and beach life in Waikiki, Hawaii, and it was a kid's dream holiday. And yet, as amazing as the trip was, it didn't run smoothly.

It was October 1, 1987, a Thursday. We were in Los Angeles, staying at the Century Plaza Hotel on the Avenue of the Stars in Century City, on the doorstep of Beverly Hills and Hollywood. The morning had started like any other. I remember the sun coming through the hotel room curtains. It was seven forty and I was awake but still in bed. Mum, my two brothers and I were in the hotel room. Dad was downstairs at a work breakfast. We were about to get ready and sort out our day. I was trying to get my morning started when the building gave a strange groan, a low, heavy sound, like something alive was shifting beneath us.

And then it hit.

The floor seemed to shudder, a sharp jolt that made me freeze, and then began to roll, as the ground had turned to liquid. The building rattled and shook; some of the furniture drawers slid open. I remember the sound most of all, not just the rumble of the quake, but the creaks of the building moving side to side, and the way everything familiar suddenly felt dangerous.

Nothing could prepare someone for an earthquake – you feel disoriented. There's an instinct to run. It is a pure fear that rises when the ground and building moves beneath your feet.

It probably lasted less than twenty seconds, but it felt endless. When it finally stopped, the silence was eerie. Not the peaceful kind – the stunned, listening silence of a city catching its breath. Somewhere down the street, an alarm or siren wailed. We had a room with a balcony, so we opened the door and went out. There were people running all over the street, it was like a Hollywood movie – ironic given we were in LA and only a few kilometres from Hollywood. A police officer looked up and saw us on the balcony and shouted, 'Don't jump!'

It seemed odd at the time, as we weren't thinking about jumping; I guess it was a scenario he had faced before.

Later that day, we learned it was a magnitude 5.9 earthquake centred near Whittier. It had initially been reported as a 6.1; Mum kept a news clipping from a paper that had been published the following day. The TV news showed images of buildings cracked, bricks littering sidewalks and closed freeways with large cracks that needed repairing. Parts of Los Angeles had been hit hard, Whittier especially, and there were casualties, damage and heartbreak. The quake occurred along a previously unrecorded sub-fault line, so while earthquakes in California are not unexpected, this one *was* somewhat unexpected. Many locals feared the worst as they were, and possibly still are, expecting a 'big one'.

For days later, there would be aftershocks, some measuring as much as 5.4. Some you didn't even feel. The Earth moving back into shape, perhaps.

Even now, decades later, I often talk about 'that time I was in an earthquake'. Earthquakes leave more than cracks in foundations and buildings. They leave impressions in the mind, moments frozen in time. That morning in Los Angeles became one of mine, a day when I felt small, but also very much alive. It became a highlight of our time in America, almost a novelty. This type of thing could have derailed the whole trip, but rather it showed a strength that was there for all to see. Sometimes things don't quite go the way they should, but it shouldn't stop you from carrying on.

At twelve, resilience doesn't feel like part of your world. You don't think of it as a strength. You just think of it as what you must do. But looking back now, I know that's exactly what it was: living through an earthquake was another example of resilience in its earliest form. We can prepare, we can plan, we can build things to code, but sometimes, life breaks through all of that and reminds us we're not in charge. That realisation didn't harden me. It softened me. It taught me to pay attention. To appreciate safety when I felt it. To be present in the moments when everything *wasn't* shaking. Easier said than done.

There's something revealing about the moment after the shaking stops. Earthquakes don't just test buildings, they test people. In the wake of an earthquake, tenacity shows itself not in the absence of fear, but in the decision to stand up again, to steady yourself amid the aftershocks, physical or emotional, and begin to rebuild.

I began to see strength in people I hadn't noticed before. In my parents, as they calmly went about their business. It was a short while before Dad was reunited with Mum and us kids. Due to the quake, the lifts were out of service, so we couldn't go up or down quickly to see each other. We most likely sensed or even assumed that each of us was safe, but you never really know. At the time, there were no mobile phones, so there was no instant contact or confirmation of what was happening. It really showed how calm my parents were, especially Mum, when it came to this type of scenario.

That morning in Los Angeles had left its mark on me, but the day was going to leave an even bigger mark in a good way. Just a few hours after the earthquake, I found myself at the gates of the happiest place on Earth, Disneyland. It was my first visit, a milestone moment, but the park's opening was delayed that morning. Following the earthquake, engineers and staff walked the park, checking every ride, every track, every cable, making sure it was still safe. The visit was part of the organised activities associated with Dad's work – we had Disney dollars to spend and were raring to go.

Eventually, the gates opened.

I remember the music playing as we stepped inside, and it plays nonstop for the whole time the park is open. The scent of popcorn and other goodies was evident. I remember how quickly I went from thinking about the morning's events to smiling and having fun. It was the start of a connection that would be enduring. To a twelve-year-old, Disneyland really is the happiest place on Earth. A standout ride was the Big Thunder Mountain Railroad, certainly not the biggest or scariest of rides, but so much fun for the whole family. A few days later, we went back again as a family, and something about those visits took root in me. Disneyland became more than a place. It became a symbol of recovery, of wonder, of togetherness. A reminder that even after the world shakes, joy can still find you.

When I had my own family, I wanted to share the same joy that I had as a child. Not a tradition as such, but a knowing that you can have a fun day out without another care in the world. And eventually I had that opportunity.

In 2003, Holly and I visited Disneyland Paris while on our honeymoon. For clarity, it wasn't the only thing we did for our honeymoon, but we had just spent 30 days driving around Europe exploring everything it has to offer. A day at Disneyland gave us an escape from the driving, and it was Holly's first time at a Disney park. It was a cold day, about two degrees. I remember we had pumpkin soup for lunch. Just a tip: don't have the soup just before you go on the Indiana Jones ride!

Two years later, when Sophie was just two years old, we visited Disneyland in Los Angeles. Watching her see it all for the first time – the colours, the characters and the endless music – felt like completing a full circle. The park I had first visited was now a place of pure joy for my daughter. In 2019, we all travelled to Walt Disney World in Orlando. Bigger, grander, wilder and yet somehow still familiar. It was another chapter, another family snapshot frozen in the amber of magic and memory. This time, it was four of us, with Josh having his first trip to the park. We did all four Disney theme parks on that trip, including a Christmas-themed night.

We returned to Disneyland Paris in 2023, older but still laughing; still chasing moments and visiting the same rides we all loved. And in 2024, we crossed the globe to Tokyo Disneyland as part of a trip to Japan. A whole new world, yet every bit as comforting. Different languages, different signs, bigger crowds, but the same smiles. The same sense of stepping out of time.

Those original Disneyland trips were some of the best moments of our time abroad as kids. That said, Dad had organised for us to spend a few nights at Waikiki in Hawaii on the way back to Australia during that first trip in 1987. We were pretty excited. Hawaii was amazing, but that part of the trip was also not without incident. We missed our flight home from Hawaii, meaning we were stuck on standby for three nights. It was certainly unplanned, but we managed to get by.

Mum and Dad handled these setbacks well. In those early years, I learnt that travel isn't always smooth, and you just need to go with the flow. Missing the flight was a mistake on their part; the flight left at 12.05am. I remember we were sitting on the beach when they worked out that we were supposed to be on the flight earlier that morning, not later that night. It must have been a horrible feeling. But they adjusted. With little money, we had to survive until we could get on a flight. Being on standby meant we had to go to the airport every day just in case seats came up. They considered several scenarios: one seat, two seats, and who would go in each scenario. Dad checked us into a cheap motel by the airport, as all the flights to Australia would leave in the middle of the night. During the day, we would just take the bus to Waikiki and enjoy the beach. After three nights, five seats became available, and we flew home. Mum and Dad never missed a flight again.

The following year, I started high school at Albany Creek State High School, which was also within walking distance of home. It's fair to say that I wasn't the greatest student academically, and I got through by doing what I had to do. A familiar comment in my report cards read along the lines of: 'Matthew would achieve better if he could apply himself.'

Nonetheless, I have some fond memories of school, and I didn't hate it; I just didn't love it. I think at that stage of my life, I didn't really know what I wanted to do, and I am not sure that I ever managed to figure that out.

I remember during high school speaking with the guidance counsellor regarding possible careers. We all had to think about what we liked and what we thought we might do. I had considered becoming a pilot. I had worked out that I could join the Australian Air Force, fly with them for the first half of my career, before joining a commercial airline. The guidance counsellor was blunt.

'You've had heart surgery; you will never be a pilot. They'll take one look at your scar on your chest and that will be that.'

I think it was the worst advice I had ever received. I don't remember being shattered, but I certainly remember feeling like school was a lost cause, and I had no backup plan or second option, so I went about my schooling without much intent, just to get through.

I got myself an after-school job at the Albany Creek Vet Clinic when a mate went on holiday and needed someone to cover for him. This was my first real job where I got paid. I was twelve and would clean out the cages of the pets who were being kept overnight, do some of the Saturday morning hydro baths for the dogs and mow the lawns when they needed doing. It was great.

When my schoolmate returned, the clinic kept me on, and I worked every second weekend. I could ride my bike to work, and I remember being paid by cheque – $10 for Saturday, $5 for Sunday, an extra $5 for the hydro bath and $10 to mow the lawn. Doesn't sound like much in today's terms, but it was the first time I learned the value of money.

I continued working at the clinic for many years; however, at the end of Year 10, our family moved to Castle Hill in Sydney. It was a big move and at a time when I was ready to complete my final two years of schooling. It caused a real academic challenge for me.

It wasn't long before I picked up some work at the North Parramatta McDonald's after my brother David started working at the same store. At the time, it was one of the busiest McDonald's in Australia and one of the first to be open 24 hours. I learnt a lot. As I settled in, I often got the graveyard shift, starting at ten in the evening and finishing at six the next morning. I'm not sure what Mum and Dad thought of that, as they would have to drop me off and pick me up, but the pay rates were better doing those odd hours. And you learn a lot about yourself doing those sorts of shifts. I think I worked out early on that I wasn't cut out for shift work.

I repeated Year 10 due to differences in the schooling system between Queensland and New South Wales before finishing Year 11 at Castle Hill State High School. Our family then moved back to Brisbane, where I completed Year 12 in 1993, a year later than my original cohort, at Albany Creek High.

While I was still in Year 12, I bought a milk run. I borrowed $10,000 to purchase the business, including the milk truck. Incredibly, it was a bank loan, and the funds were borrowed on the basis that the business would earn enough money to pay it off. I look back at that time now and shake my head. *What was I thinking borrowing that much money at such a young age?* It seems like a lot for someone still at school. But it worked out. The milk run covered large parts of Albany Creek. By then, the industry had been deregulated, so the milk runs weren't worth as much as they might have been previously. Essentially, the price I paid was for the truck and a small amount to take on the established run. It was still a good run, and I delivered to thirty per cent of the houses in the area; the average across Brisbane was less than half that.

I worked hard, but it made me good money, more than I would have got working casually in hospitality or retail. After about eighteen months, I had paid off the loan. At that stage, the run still included milk in six-hundred-millimetre glass bottles; these were easily the best sellers. Blue tops were for full-cream milk, red tops for trim or skim and gold for unhomogenised milk with the cream on top.

When I took on the run, it was five afternoons a week. I was keen to change it to three days to suit any future university studies I might undertake. It would also cut down my running costs a little. I put a survey out to my customers, on a little paper slip, asking for their preferences on future delivery. While I received a range of responses, the majority supported reducing delivery days. I put together a newsletter thanking everyone for their feedback, and the results from my survey showed that most customers preferred delivery three days a week. I rescheduled the run to suit my needs and it worked. I didn't lose any customers. This was a great lesson in the value of consultation. I know some customers wanted a different outcome or different days, but they felt valued as they had the chance to contribute and input into the outcome.

When I finished school, my OP (overall position) score wasn't good enough to automatically enter university to study leisure management. Following the poor advice from the guidance counsellor, I had decided partway through Year 12 that leisure management was a study goal that I could look forward to. To help me improve my OP, I did a year of

TAFE studying an Associate Diploma in Business Management. The study was useful as it gave me some credit towards a degree, but didn't overly challenge me. Perhaps I could have challenged myself more; I seemed to cruise through school without really trying, and the business management course was the same. While I was cruising, I was still working hard, running the milk run. The year at TAFE did the trick, and the following year I enrolled at Griffith University to complete a Bachelor of Arts in Leisure Management, majoring in sport and tourism management. The degree was fun; again, I was cruising but seemed to be doing well enough not to want to try harder. I had always thought that I would end up in a full-time job by the end of the degree, but I still didn't really know where.

Blending study with the milk run meant long days – up to twenty hours. Ultimately, I couldn't sustain this, and it took its toll on me. I remember one day breaking down completely, just crying and not knowing what to do or what was going on. At the time, I went to the family doctor, who I had been seeing since I was born. He prescribed me diazepam. I wasn't really interested in diazepam; I had heard bad things about it, and it was an addictive drug. My grandmother on Dad's side was somewhat addicted to the drug and would ask her friends who worked at the hospital to bring some home for her. It was a telling moment for me, as even though I needed help, I didn't want to take the medication. I took one tablet and ended up throwing the rest in the bin.

I decided to see another doctor who prescribed me dosulepin. He told me that I had a 'condition' that older people get. He said it was a little unusual to see it in people my age, but if you take the drug, things will get better. And to a certain extent, they did, but I was run down, and when I look back, I was suffering from burnout. I learned later that dosulepin is a tricyclic antidepressant used to treat depression. The doctor believed that I had reduced serotonin levels, and the drug would increase serotonin in the brain and therefore improve my mood. One of the things

I remember is that I was told it was not addictive. I could start on a lower dose, increasing each week, and once I felt better, I could then decrease each week until I was off it.

Although it seemed to work, I didn't really like taking the drug; I thought I needed to slow down somehow. So, I put the feelers out for someone to take on the milk run, and within a week or two, I had a buyer. After all, it was a successful business. The buyer had another milk run and this would be the perfect addition to his existing business. So, we agreed to the terms and I sold. Essentially, I sold the business for the same price I paid for it. Because the industry was deregulated, it wasn't worth anything as such and was difficult to increase in value. However, because I had paid out the loan, I now had a small sum of funds that I could lock away and put towards a deposit on a house. Not long after selling, I could feel the health benefits, so, with the support of the doctor I stopped taking the medication by gradually reducing the dose. I remember thinking that I should never work myself that hard again; sometimes I need to keep reminding myself of that.

During my degree, I completed two industry practicums. The first was with a company called Wild Escapes, where we took guided kayak trips, mostly on the Brisbane River, some in the city and out near Fernvale in the upper reaches of the river. It was great and something I really enjoyed, but not the career I was looking for.

The second practicum was a placement within the Queensland Government working with the Office of Sport. This was in 1997, and the organisation of the placement was very structured compared to Wild Escapes. Despite being a volunteer placement, we were required to undertake a written application and an interview. We all got placements, and it was an excellent experience for university students. I was placed in the infrastructure team. On the day I arrived, we were given an induction and an overview of the type of work we would be doing before being taken to our respective teams. I will still never forget the day I was introduced to my supervisor.

She looked at me and then looked at her supervisor and said, 'I told you I didn't want one of those students, I put all that paperwork in the bin.' It wasn't personal; however my supervisor was not impressed that I had arrived. It was a welcome I didn't expect.

Despite this, they took me in and gave me a project to work on – the National Sport and Recreation Facilities Plan. I was given a desk, a computer to use and introduced to a few people who could help me pull it together. Looking back, this was where my career started.

Over the ten weeks of the practicum, I attended the office in the city two days a week. I managed to pull together, with the help of my colleagues, summaries of every major sport and what their needs were in Queensland. The bones of the document were written for someone to finish off and produce.

At the end of the placement, we were offered casual work to support the department's stand at the Royal Queensland Show, otherwise known as Brisbane's Ekka. My official first day of paid work was August 7, 1998, working at the sport and recreation stand in the Queensland Government pavilion. Our stand was focused on the Queensland Academy of Sport and somewhat interactive. Visitors could stand on a mat (that was connected to a computer) and try to jump as high as possible. On landing on the mat, a computer program would calculate how high you had jumped. Great for kids and a bit of a gimmick. Thinking back to that time, when computers were still very much in their infancy, this was high tech. Especially when you consider that in the office we weren't yet using emails – we were still printing memos and using fax machines to communicate.

Following the work at the Ekka, I was contracted two days a week to finish the National Facilities Sport and Recreation Plan. You could say that this was my first real job and a great project to work on. I was finishing university and working professionally two days a week in a nine-to-five job. I was busy but not burned out. By the end of 1997, the project was ending and the drafting had finished. Following a short break over Christmas, I was invited back to the office to finalise publication and for the launch by the then minister. It was a great piece of work to put on my resume.

During those closing stages, an advisor's job was advertised. There were two positions, one in Warwick and one in Dalby. I had been encouraged to apply, so I did. I wasn't sure that I wanted to move to either of those places, but I applied, nonetheless. My resume and letter were good, but as a university leaver, it wasn't great. I had no real job experience, just the milk run and some casual jobs I had done. I think I was offered an interview due to my involvement and commitment. I figured that I was probably making up the numbers, and the interview experience would be great practice for me. The interviews were in the city, so off I went. I have to say, I thought I interviewed well; however, at first, I didn't hear anything. Several weeks went by and nothing. Eventually, I got a phone call – I wasn't successful for either job in Warwick or Dalby. However, there was another opening in Charleville, and I was offered that role. This was obviously not what I was expecting, so I explained that I needed to think about it and offered to get back to them the next day. I got off the phone and thought to myself, *Where the heck is Charleville?*

Back in 1997, googling wasn't a thing. So, I got a map out and found where Charleville was– around 750 kilometres from Brisbane. I tried to find what I could about the region but didn't come up with much. No real info on housing, food, climate, anything. Despite this, I rang the department back and said I'd take the position. I had nothing to lose, and I had just received my first real full-time job.

I got the chance to take a trip out that way to look at some houses and meet some key people. I got the bus out and drove back to Toowoomba with a staff member from the Toowoomba office. I'll never forget the bus trip out to Charleville. The night before, I had attended a Metallica concert at the Brisbane Entertainment Centre. It was a terrific gig, but incredibly loud. From memory, the band was fined for being over the allowable noise level. My ears were ringing the whole way out on the bus trip the next day. I think it took a few days before my ears settled down and I could hear properly again.

That first trip to Charleville was a success. The town itself was beautiful and the surrounding countryside was in full bloom. I just remember everything being so green and full of life. I had been fortunate to visit following a larger-than-average rainfall for that season, so rather than drought, it was somewhat lush. I found a place to rent and moved out a few weeks later. I remember thinking rent was expensive; it didn't seem that much cheaper than in the urban areas. I initially had a house for $130 a week, then moved into a unit for $95 a week. To put it in perspective, my job paid around $37,000 a year.

Charleville was a great place to live and an even better place to cut my teeth working with the local councils and sport and recreation clubs. It also marked the first time email addresses were rolled out to all staff. I clearly remember that I was allowed to dial up once a day to download my emails, then had to disconnect so I didn't rack up a huge bill. If anything was urgent, you still had to send a fax!

Some of the job was a little out of the ordinary. I had a weekly session on the local radio and was regularly interviewed for the local newspaper – neither of which would be allowed in government these days. I would get asked about all sorts of things – local sport, Queensland, Australia, even about the Commonwealth Games that were on that year. I was an invited guest at the School of the Air or the School of Distance Education, teaching country kids about the ins and outs of sport, communicated over the radio waves to kids on properties across southwest Queensland.

Overall, it was a fun job, but it was a long way from home and a long way from the coast. So, when an opening came up in the Warwick office roughly six months later, I took it and relocated.

Warwick was a different place again. While it wasn't close to the coast either, I could at least head back to Brisbane most weekends or visit either the Gold Coast or Sunshine Coast. Work was different again, and it was another great learning experience for me. In a short space of time, I learnt so much about the industry I was working in through my experiences in both Charleville and Warwick. These experiences set me up for a long career in the industry.

It's funny how life works. In 1999, while in Warwick, I opened my front door to a new flatmate and ended up with a spouse!

People often ask how I met Holly, and the truth is, it wasn't anything dramatic or exciting. No lightning bolts. No grand gestures. Just two people crossing paths in Warwick, Queensland. Holly moved in as a flatmate when the flatmate I had moved back to Brisbane. Holly had just accepted a job in Warwick. That's it. We shared a house. Nothing fancy. A simple setup. A few bedrooms, a dodgy couch and a kitchen that was well used.

At first, we were just housemates, which allowed us to become friends. I think I liked her early on, but if I'm being honest, I'm pretty sure her mum liked me more than she did. Holly took a bit longer to come around. But I didn't mind. We had time. There was no pressure. We got to know each other slowly, shared groceries, took turns cooking dinner and watched TV together. There was something about Holly, though; calm, smart, kind and in her own way funny. The more time we spent together, the more I realised she wasn't just a flatmate. She was the person I wanted to see at the end of every day.

Eventually, something shifted. We stopped being just friends and started becoming something more. The line between flatmates and partners blurred until one day, we were dating. And after that, it just kept going forward. Except I moved away from Warwick, and ultimately so did Holly, which put the relationship on pause temporarily.

As much as I enjoyed living and working in Charleville and Warwick, I missed being closer to the beach lifestyle. When I was younger, particularly during our holidays to Caloundra, I always said I wanted to live by the beach. Happily, that is what I ended up doing. After a couple of years in Warwick, I applied for a job as a sport planning officer at Caboolture, and after a rather lengthy recruitment process, I was successful. I remember Dad and I looking at a couple of cheap rental properties in and around Caboolture without much luck, so I decided to rent in Maroochydore and commute each day. This was in 2000, and it was the first time I lived on the Sunshine Coast. I have lived there ever since.

Ultimately, Holly moved to the Sunshine Coast as well, and we ended up renting a place in Buderim. In some respects, Holly and I did things as a couple out of order, but they seem to work out well for us in the long run. We were both sick of paying rent and worked out quickly that we could get a mortgage for less than the cost of renting. So, we went ahead and bought a house in Buderim. It was a three-bedroom property and cost us $192,000. I remember the bank at the time telling us we were eligible for a loan of over $440,000 and I couldn't understand how anyone in their right mind would want to borrow that much money.

In the end, it was the perfect decision and place for us to start our union and start a family. We then got engaged, and eventually, on September 20, 2003, we were standing side by side at our wedding. We married at the beachside suburb of Mooloolaba in beautiful weather at Charles Clarke Park. The reception was held upstairs in the function room at the Mooloolaba Surf Life Saving Club. It was a terrific reception that left us with lots of fond memories. We flew out a few days later for our honeymoon to Europe. Thirty days driving around Europe was amazing and a great first test of our marriage. I remember using a road atlas to get our way around; there were no navigation systems or smartphones to help us!

Our first child, Sophie, was born in July 2006 and her brother Joshua arrived in April 2009. The house we had bought in Buderim was perfect for our small family; however, in 2010, we bought land and built a house that we moved into in 2011 and have lived in since. Holly and I have come a long way since those early days as flatmates in Warwick, building a life together that neither of us could have imagined back then. We endured many challenges that you would expect as a young couple and a young family. However, our biggest and most defining moments, which would come after July 2014, could never have been predicted.

Living with an unspeakable tragedy

I remember seeing a Facebook post from the day of the tragedy. It was a photo of the Australian and Queensland flags at half-mast at the Mooloolaba Surf Life Saving Club, where I was a member. While I cannot remember the exact words that accompanied the image, they were along the lines of, 'Flags at half-mast in memory of those who didn't make it back to Earth.' To this day, I can't believe that the flags were lowered in honour of my parents.

How do you live with an unspeakable tragedy? Well, the short answer is, initially, you don't. You feel like you are struggling to survive. It's something you can't learn; the only way to know how you would react is to experience it, and it's not something recommended in a general sense. There's no 'getting over it'. And, in those early days, you learn to carry it with you because you can't get rid of it. Over time, you can find a way to have it sit with you, but it is still there. Some days you shoulder it more easily. Other days, it presses against your forehead or chest like a weight you didn't ask for and can't put down.

In a word, it's simply exhausting.

There's no tidy sequence of emotions when you lose someone suddenly, violently and without warning, especially not in something as public, political and brutal as MH17. The grief isn't neat. It's chaotic. It comes in waves that knock you down when you least expect it. And in those early days, the waves don't stop coming.

There is no doubt that I was in shock, a kind of numb disbelief. *It doesn't feel real.* You hear the news, but your mind can't catch up. *How can something like this happen? How can this be my story now? This is something that happens to other people.*

There is sadness, anger, guilt and fear. There is no order, no way of knowing what will come next. Different things trigger different emotions. For example, in those early days, I would only need to see a car like Dad's, or a caravan or a plane, and I would immediately feel that sense of sadness and loss. For many months, I didn't think I would get past some of that, but over time, it improves, although it never really goes away. There would be times when I would just cry, perhaps triggered by something, although for most of the time it would be for no reason, just because I was sad. As someone who didn't necessarily cry much, I initially found myself uneasy at the outpouring of such emotion.

In those early days, the anger can be raw, burning. An anger directed at the people responsible. At the world for allowing it. At governments. At war. At strangers who don't seem to understand. It comes back when there is a high-profile event, such as the annual anniversary or a court case. There might be increased media attention that is hard to escape; it would be easy to ignore the media articles, but I find myself drawn to them in case something is written about my parents.

Alongside anger comes a deep, hollow sadness, not just for what's been taken but for everything that will never happen now. All the future moments erased, things weren't supposed to be like this; we had so much more to discover together. The birthdays. The conversations. The ordinary, precious days that should have been. This hurts the most when I think about my children and what they have missed out on. My parents were wonderful grandparents, and my children simply didn't deserve to go through all of this.

There's guilt, too. Survivor's guilt. Guilt for still being here. Guilt for not trying to stop it. I mean, how would I have stopped it? But even though logically there is nothing I could have done to prevent this, it doesn't mean you don't wonder *what if I did…*

I have even found myself consumed by guilt for the small relief I sometimes feel when life demands my attention and gives me a moment's break from the grief – if you catch yourself doing this, it is the worst feeling, you feel guilty. That first day, I felt guilty breaking into Mum and Dad's house without their permission; the guilt was immediate.

And then there's fear. Fear of what comes next. Fear of forgetting. Fear of being forgotten. Sometimes you *do* get forgotten; the rest of the world doesn't stop, it keeps moving. Fear of living a life that now feels unrecognisable without my parents in it.

I remember waking up the first morning after. I felt terrible, exhausted, despite having had some sleep. It was a feeling that would repeat itself for weeks to come. I looked outside – the sun was shining, the birds were chirping, it was a beautiful day. The world was still moving. I checked the news just in case I had it all wrong. *Nope, my world is still buggered.* My headache hadn't gone away. It was a Saturday, no school, so everyone was home.

The kids need breakfast. I should probably help sort that out. I got up and tried to start the day. It was a pattern that happened a fair bit in those early days, but I always felt like I needed to do something. Some days were better than others. In many regards, having younger children was all the motivation I needed to get up and start my day. I remember telling myself that it was okay to be sad and upset, but it wasn't okay to stay in bed and do nothing. I think that helped me get up and do something. Of course, it would be perfectly fine to stay in bed on some occasions, just for me not to make a habit of it.

Looking back, what helped in those early days was the dossier Dad had sent me. It helped on that first day when I felt like I was breaking into Mum and Dad's house. But it also provided one very basic instruction that set the course ahead for us to take care of my parents' affairs.

In bold writing, it read: 'On death, notify Susi O'Reilly immediately. Also, let Perry Wilkey know.'

I remember reading this before my parents left for their trip. It was a bit hard to read when they were alive; it's not something you really want to think about. And to be honest, I didn't really care who Susi or Perry were, so I paid little attention to it, until it became real. I can tell you, it is harder to read when it happens, on death, that is.

Susi was Mum and Dad's solicitor, who had copies of both their wills in safekeeping, and Perry looked after their superannuation. I did exactly as it said and rang both. I have to say it made those first few moments much easier. It was as if Dad was talking to me and guiding me through the process, and my instinct was to listen to what was being said. After all, Dad had done all the work and put the pieces in place, should something like this happen. It was logical that I follow it.

And while in that moment, there were a lot of things we couldn't do because we didn't have the bodies and therefore didn't have a death certificate, it gave us direction and a path forward when we needed it most.

Dad, ever the planner, was always organised, but this was and still is a great life lesson in always being ready for your passing.

It kind of goes without saying, but you really do feel helpless in this situation. Not only are you grieving, but you want to help or do something useful, and you simply cannot.

In the immediate days after MH17 was downed, when the world seemed to blur with shock, disbelief and confusion, there were people who stepped forward with strength and unwavering purpose. For my family and for many others, DFAT became our steady point of contact in the chaos. Following my first phone call with them that morning, we were assigned a liaison officer who would call us every day.

Our contact was calm, compassionate and relentlessly focused on keeping us informed, even when information was frustratingly scarce, sometimes changing by the hour, or painful to hear. We also knew there was a team of people behind the scenes supporting the progress. They didn't try to soften the truth. They respected the dignity of our situation. In a time when trust was hard to come by, DFAT earned it through the simple acts of listening, updating and following through.

Alongside them were the Australian Federal Police (AFP), who took on the heavy burden of supporting families, guiding the DNA and repatriation process, the early stages and ongoing investigation and liaising with international counterparts. The AFP also allocated us liaison officers – police officers who would contact us regularly, but not daily, and would meet and visit in person, always at our house at a time that suited us. Their work was profound, matching DNA, piecing together identities, escorting remains and standing with families through unspeakable moments. The same officers stayed with us right through to the criminal trial. They didn't just treat this as a crime to be solved; they treated it as a responsibility owed to the dead and to those of us left behind.

Looking back, I don't think words like 'government support' fully capture what DFAT and AFP gave us in those early days. They gave us something rarer – a sense of being seen, heard and cared for at a time when the world felt impossibly large and our grief impossibly small.

Most importantly, they were enabled through strong leadership within the government to provide support. They didn't have all the answers. No one did. It was much more than support; they stood beside us, and that mattered more than they probably knew.

When this tragedy first happened, my instinct was to go to the crash site. An instinct perhaps, but I wanted to see it for myself, verify in a way what happened, collect Mum and Dad's remains so that I could bring them home, even help with the investigation and clean up. The logistics of all of this didn't even enter my head; I just needed to do something, that's what I kept telling myself. It is a weird feeling. I was not the only one drawn to this; my brothers were too.

With David in London, geographically, he was closest to Ukraine. He could potentially duck over to Kyiv and represent our family. But my instinct was telling me that travelling to Ukraine wasn't a good idea, it was not safe and would not help one bit. The crash site itself was in a brewing conflict, controlled by separatist groups. This instinct was the same advice the AFP had given us: there was no way to guarantee the safety of anyone who went. And for David, being in Ukraine on his own without any support from family or friends nearby would have been one of the worst things to do.

And so, the three of us ended up together on the Sunshine Coast. My brothers and I have always gotten on well together, but this would surely test us living together again under the same roof after spending many years apart. In the end it all happened quickly, we were together within 48 hours of Mum and Dad passing away. I will never forget the moment David walked through the arrival doors of the Brisbane International Airport. He was escorted through by one of the airline staff, who had looked after him all the way from London. He was a broken man. Exhausted and tired, having endured the long-haul flight following the horrific death of our parents just a day or two earlier. It was an emotional reunion, but not in the way a reunion should be. I am still incredibly proud of David for making that trip under those circumstances.

For that night, I had booked a room in north Brisbane for the three of us to stay in. It was nothing flash, just a small apartment. We probably could have stayed at Mum and Dad's place but making that decision was initially difficult. Staying there without their permission almost didn't feel right.

At that time, various media outlets had been visiting Mum and Dad's place to stake it out for people to make comments, so we were careful in those early days to avoid some of that attention. We went to the apartment to try to get some sleep so we could have the energy to start unravelling what had happened. We didn't really sleep; we woke early and ended up at the nearby McDonald's for a coffee and some breakfast. The printed newspapers were available for reading; the front-page news was all about MH17, another painful reminder of why the three of us were together. It was just for the one night and ultimately, we made our way back to my house on the Sunshine Coast where we lived together for weeks.

The house was big enough for all of us, however, we didn't really have adequate bedding for longer stays. Our neighbours were fantastic and lent us beds and other items for as long as we needed, which meant everyone was as comfortable as could be. The generosity of others was always on display at this time. People lent us their cars, offered to help pay for things or gave us money to get by. It was incredible, and I always tried to remember to thank people, but I'm sure sometimes I didn't. I was just too preoccupied with the matters at hand.

In the days following the tragedy, there was an outpouring of kindness from friends, neighbours and even strangers. Cards and flowers arrived steadily, people wanting to say they were sorry, to let us know we were in their thoughts. The flowers seemed endless. Within a few days, we had more than twenty bouquets in the house. Our house looked less like a home and more like a florist's shopfront, except we didn't have enough vases to put them all in. They were in buckets, jugs, bottles, anything we could find to keep them going. The gesture was beautiful. It meant something, yet grief has a strange way of making even kindness feel overwhelming.

What I hadn't anticipated was how this sea of sympathy would affect me and other members of my family physically. I've suffered from hay fever and allergies most of my life, and one morning I woke up barely able to open my eyes. My throat felt thick, raw, as though it were closing over. In the middle of such deep sadness, it was absurd in a way, suffocating, quite literally, under the weight of people's good intentions. I remember standing in the middle of the room, surrounded by flowers, thinking how even grief finds ways to be complicated. It wasn't the flowers' fault. It wasn't anyone's fault. But even kindness had its side effects. To counter this, I ended up putting all the flowers outside; it seemed wrong, but I felt it was the only solution at the time. For the most part it worked, along with taking an antihistamine.

That's something they don't tell you about loss – it's never just emotional. It creeps into your body, your sleep, even the air you breathe.

I remember waking up on the Monday after the downing, early, worried about Mum and Dad's stuff that was in Ukraine somewhere. I thought about all sorts of things, including Dad's camera, my parents' phones, but more distressingly at the time, their wallet with credit cards and the like. Even in those early days, we had heard stories of personal effects being stolen and things like credit cards being used in Ukraine. It was an unstable place, so looting certainly wasn't out of the question. I grabbed Dad's dossier, and he had all his banking account numbers listed for us, including credit cards. In those early hours of Monday morning, I rang the bank to cancel the credit cards.

A polite, helpful lady answered. Initially, the answer was, of course, 'No. You can't cancel someone else's credit cards, especially over the phone with no documentation.' I was doing my best to be polite back but was getting nowhere. So, for the first time, I was frank about our situation and simply said, 'My parents were killed onboard MH17, and I need to cancel their credit cards before someone starts using them in Ukraine.'

I was stunned. I couldn't believe what I just said. It all sounded a bit surreal, something that happens to other people, but it was the truth. There was silence on the other end of the phone. I waited a few more moments.

'Are you still there?'

I heard crying on the other end of the phone. I didn't mean to make anyone cry, but it was the gravity of the situation. She was so apologetic and sympathetic for me, but there was nothing she could do to help – except maybe cancel those credit cards. In the end, her solution was perfect; she was able to put a hold on the credit cards for forty-eight hours, which gave me enough time to get to the bank in person with the appropriate documentation to put something in place more permanently. Most importantly, it meant that the cards could not be used.

Over time, we learnt that my stress over the credit cards was probably warranted; there were examples of other family members being caught out with inappropriate use of cards, phones and other valuables. All distressing and annoying for those families at a time when it wasn't needed.

One thing I couldn't change was the media scrutiny, which felt relentless in those first days and weeks after MH17. No matter how hard we tried to shield ourselves from it, it was everywhere – on the news, in the papers, online, filling every screen and headline. I made a conscious effort to avoid being drawn into it because I knew what we needed most was accurate, clear information, something the media simply didn't have.

Speculation, blame, rumour, it wasn't helping anyone. It certainly wasn't helping us.

But even with that intention, it was impossible to fully turn away. This was the biggest story in the world for days, if not weeks, and somehow, impossibly, it involved my Mum and Dad. We found ourselves watching, reading, listening, not because we trusted what was being said, but because it felt like the only connection we had to what was happening. Even through the noise, we were desperate for scraps of truth. It is also hard to turn away when you see photos of your parents continually being plastered across the news.

The real problem wasn't the reporting itself; it was the media's hunger for a headline, for something provocative. They weren't interested in grief. They weren't interested in heartbreak. They wanted anger, outrage, someone to point a finger and say, 'We blame Russia! We're coming after them!' That's what sold. That's what made the front pages. But none of that captured what we were feeling. We weren't driven by politics or revenge. We just missed our parents and grandparents. In that heartbreak, the media's noise felt not just unhelpful, it felt cruel.

I drew on my work experience and prepared a media release. It was very plain but thanked everyone for their support and asked for privacy while we were grieving. It became a useful piece of paper, and it meant that I couldn't really say anything that I might regret later. I could give the media something and they would leave us to grieve.

In one of the more extreme examples, in those first two days, a TV reporter and camera crew turned up at our house. I answered the door, and the reporter asked me how I was feeling, and the camera was rolling. The kids were in the background; the last thing I wanted was for them to be on TV. I was shocked and angry that they would do such a thing. I could have easily gone off and said something I'd regret, exactly what they wanted. I grabbed my media release, gave it to him and didn't say a word. I was so annoyed by the invasion of privacy, but at the same time, I was proud of how I handled it; they missed out on my story that day.

The relationship with the media improved over time, and overall, they respected my privacy. You could say they were just doing their job, and I know that most journalists would prefer to do so under better circumstances. Ultimately, I would speak with various media but only when the outlet was prepared to share a genuine story and when I was ready and comfortable to speak.

The phone calls in those few days were endless. Understandably, I was receiving calls from family and friends, but also, I was receiving calls from both Australian and international authorities, lawyers looking for business, people claiming to represent the airline and the national and international media.

I have never had that many phone calls ever. In the first few hours, I unplugged the landline rather than continually answering the phone or having other family members answer it. I would check the messages every day or so, and if it were someone important, I would get back to them. I left my mobile on and would screen the calls. A lot of calls were from no caller ID. If I weren't expecting a call, I would let it go to voicemail and return the call if I needed to. Screening no caller ID became a little tricky as many of the official calls from the AFP and government departments would be from private numbers; however, I stuck to the idea that if the call was important, they would find a way to get to me.

A few days after the incident, I went to the gym. Holly was getting some physio on her leg, which she had injured several weeks before. I have always enjoyed being active but was not much of a gym-goer. It was exercise, nonetheless, and I recall telling myself it was good for me.

While I was on the treadmill, my mobile phone rang. No caller ID. For some reason, I answered it, rather than screening the call. I was tired, cranky and quite frankly getting shitty with all these people wanting a piece of my time. I answered rudely and abruptly.

'Hello!'

'Ah, hello, is this Matthew Horder?'

'Yes, it is. Who am I speaking with and what do you want?'

'Ahhh, Matthew, it's Tony Abbott here. I wanted to speak with you about your parents.'

I immediately hopped off the treadmill and headed outside to take the call.

Tony Abbott was the Prime Minister of Australia at the time. We had been given notice that he might call, but I was still not expecting it. *Why would the Prime Minister want to talk to me? Surely, he has better things to do.* In many ways, it highlighted the gravity and scale of our situation. The Prime Minister had called every Australian family who was affected by MH17, a big commitment for a busy person. It was a call that helped immensely as I knew we had support at the highest level, and it set the path for many things to follow in the days, months and years ahead.

We talked for about twenty minutes. Tony was genuine and empathetic. He asked about my family; more importantly, he asked me about my parents. I'm not sure where it came from, but I told Tony that my parents were good, hard-working Australians. They had never asked for anything from their country, but now more than ever, they needed help. Tony was very clear.

'We cannot bring them back, but we will bring them home, as far as we humanly can.'

This set the tone for what was to come; it was true leadership that enabled multiple government departments to operationalise to deliver on the needs of all families. It was also a side of Tony Abbott not seen in public, and at a time when we felt helpless, we had a small sense of hope that Mum and Dad might be found and we could bring them home.

In the end, Tony Abbott's response to MH17 was immediate and forceful; it would also be enduring. In those first days of shock and disbelief, it really did matter to hear the country's leader call it what it was: a crime, not just a tragedy. Under his leadership, Australia secured a unanimous United Nations resolution, demanding justice for the victims and their families. He sent Australian personnel into a war zone to help recover our loved ones and made it clear to the world, Russia included, that we would not simply let this go. Politics aside, what mattered most to families like mine was knowing that our government stood behind us, that our parents' deaths were not being reduced to a footnote in some far-off conflict. Abbott's bluntness wasn't always diplomatic, but in those days, it was exactly what many of us needed to hear.

When I wrapped up the phone call with Tony, he asked me if there was anything else he could do to help in the meantime. I don't know why, but I relayed the story of the media outlet that turned up at our front door with a reporter and camera. I asked if there was anything he could do to stop it.

He didn't hesitate.

'Leave it with me, I will ask one of my staff to follow up with them.'

To this day, I have not heard from that media outlet.

Resolution 2166

In the days that followed the downing of MH17, I came to understand just how complex the world of international politics really is. News reports kept mentioning the United Nations, an organisation I'd always known in theory but never truly paid much attention to. I never really had to. The United Nations exists to bring countries together, to try to prevent wars, protect human rights and offer humanitarian support. It's meant to be the base from which nations set aside their differences to work for something bigger than themselves: peace.

At the heart of the UN is the Security Council, made up of fifteen countries tasked with maintaining global peace and security. Among them, five countries hold permanent seats and special veto powers: the United States, the United Kingdom, France, China and Russia. The other ten member nations rotate every two years. The Security Council, based in New York City, is one of six organs of the UN and any resolutions made by the Security Council are legally binding in international law. In the wake of MH17, the Security Council was called upon to act because what had happened was an international crime with political consequences stretching far beyond the wreckage in a Ukrainian field.

Just four days after the crash, the Security Council passed Resolution 2166. It was a rare moment of unity. Even Russia, under intense scrutiny, didn't veto the resolution. The resolution called for a full, thorough and independent investigation. It demanded that those responsible be held accountable and that families like mine be treated with dignity and respect. More importantly, the resolution paved the way for access to the site, to recover the human remains in a respectful and dignified way and to enable a proper investigation to occur. At home, far from New York or Kyiv, those formal words on paper felt oddly personal. It wasn't just politics; it was a recognition, from the highest level, that what had happened mattered. That our parents mattered. That accountability mattered.

One of the figures who stood out to me during those days was Julie Bishop, Australia's Foreign Affairs Minister at the time. In the often-cold world of international diplomacy, she brought a sharpness, a strength and a sense of moral clarity that cut through the usual diplomatic language. I watched as she addressed the United Nations Security Council with conviction and precision, demanding justice not just for Australia's thirty-eight citizens but for every life lost on board MH17. She spoke calmly but forcefully, making it clear that this was not just a matter of politics; it was a matter of humanity. Further, Julie was instrumental in ensuring Russia voted in favour of the resolution. Julie had met with the Russian delegate on the morning of the vote to convince him to vote in favour and not veto the resolution.

In a sea of international voices, it meant something to hear someone speak directly for us, for Mum, for Dad, for the families who hadn't asked to be thrust into this kind of global spotlight. Julie's words made it clear that we weren't invisible, and that what had happened to our loved ones wouldn't be quietly forgotten or pushed aside for diplomatic convenience.

It also gave me a completely new appreciation and understanding of the United Nations and the Security Council.

It was a strange comfort, knowing that in the halls of the United Nations, amid the flags and protocols, someone was fighting to ensure that truth, justice and dignity weren't lost beneath the politics. For all its limitations, Resolution 2166 was a line drawn in the sand. It acknowledged our grief and, more importantly, it demanded accountability from those who caused it.

Over the years, I have learnt more about what Resolution 2166 meant in terms of the recovery of our parents' bodies and the various legal investigations. I have learnt more about the United Nations and what the Security Council means in world affairs; it's certainly not perfect, but it's a starting place on global terms.

Following the successful passing of Resolution 2166, we received a phone call from Julie. Just like the Prime Minister, she had been contacting all the Australian families, and this time it was our turn. Julie had just left the United Nations headquarters and boarded a flight, ready to depart for Amsterdam.

I clearly remember the phone call. I was in the car with my two brothers, which was perfect, it meant we could all be part of the conversation. As with the Prime Minister, it was somewhat surreal that the Minister for Foreign Affairs was contacting us, but we had already been dealing with the Department of Foreign Affairs, and we needed their help. Julie must have given us about twenty minutes of her time as well.

We could hear in the background the preflight procedures, other passengers boarding the flight, the safety briefing and everything else that goes with it. Julie kept talking to us the whole time, even when the flight attendant asked her to hang up, she kept talking. She was focused on representing the families and looking after the interests of Australia and our loved ones. She spoke so compassionately, and we immediately felt at ease; we had an ally in a world we knew nothing about.

Julie confidently described everything she had just done and achieved at the United Nations Security Council. We didn't immediately understand the gravity of what she achieved, but it was exactly what we needed to hear in that moment. Those first few days were frustrating, as there was limited information and updates, so hearing there was some progress through the Security Council was a small relief.

We couldn't understand why there wasn't an immediate investigation and recovery of bodies, how we were caught up in a conflict that had nothing to do with Mum, Dad or ourselves. None of it made sense. But through Resolution 2166, Julie paved the way forward. Above everything else, after negotiations, she was able to convince the Russian delegate to support the resolution. He could have vetoed it, given that Russia actively supporting the separatists occupying Eastern Ukraine at the time.

This phone call was the beginning of a connection that would continue for many years. Julie was unprecedented in the way she treated our family, and I am sure many other families. And it was on a personal level – she provided us with her private phone number and said to contact her at any time if we needed anything from the department. It was leadership of the highest level. This direction, in turn, ultimately empowered her department to respond in the most appropriate way, which meant we never really needed to call Julie; we would get access to everything we needed anyway.

In 2019, I was able to travel to the United States of America with my family, and while we were in New York, I booked us on a tour of the United Nations. In the past, I would not have considered this type of tour, as I would have found it boring, but given the circumstances with my parents, I found it incredibly fascinating and wanted to show it to my children and speak to them about it. We pretty much got to see everything within the United Nations headquarters. All chambers for the six organs – General Assembly, the Economics and Social Council, the Trusteeship Council, the

International Court of Justice, the Secretariat and, of course, the Security Council. None of the functions were in session, so we got to go into every room. When we got to the Security Council, I felt quite emotional. To anyone else, it was just a room, but it felt so much more than that to me. I took the kids and explained what Julie Bishop did for us in that room, how she convinced Russia to vote in favour of the resolution and what it meant for their grandparents and all of us.

Resolution 2166, as published by the United Nations Security Council, says:[1]

Resolution 2166 (2014)

Adopted by the Security Council at its 7221st meeting, on 21 July 2014

The Security Council,

Deploring the downing of a civilian aircraft on an international flight, Malaysia Airlines flight MH17, on 17 July in Donetsk Oblast, Ukraine, with the loss of all 298 passengers and crew on board,

Reaffirming the rules of international law that prohibit acts of violence that pose a threat to the safety of international civil aviation and emphasizing the importance of holding those responsible for violations of these rules to account,

Recalling its press statement of 18 July 2014,

Stressing the need for a full, thorough and independent international investigation into the incident in accordance with international civil aviation guidelines, noting in this regard the crucial role played by the International Civil Aviation Organization (ICAO) in aircraft accident and incident investigations, and welcoming the decision by ICAO to send a team to work in coordination with the Ukrainian National Bureau of Incidents and Accidents Investigation of Civil Aircraft in this investigation, following a request for assistance by Ukraine to ICAO and others,

Expressing serious concern that armed groups in Ukraine have impeded immediate, safe, secure and unrestricted access to the crash site and the surrounding area for the appropriate investigating authorities, the Organization for Security and Cooperation in Europe (OSCE) Special Monitoring Mission in Ukraine and representatives of other relevant international organizations assisting the investigation in accordance with ICAO and other established procedures,

1. Condemns in the strongest terms the downing of Malaysia Airlines flight MH17 on 17 July in Donetsk Oblast, Ukraine, resulting in the tragic loss of 298 lives;

2. Reiterates its deepest sympathies and condolences to the families of the victims of this incident and to the people and governments of the victims' countries of origin;

3. Supports efforts to establish a full, thorough and independent international investigation into the incident in accordance with international civil aviation guidelines;

4. Recognizes the efforts under way by Ukraine, working in coordination with ICAO and other international experts and organizations, including representatives of States of Occurrence, Registry, Operator, Design and Manufacture, as well as States who have lost nationals on MH17, to institute an international investigation of the incident, and calls on all States to provide any requested assistance to civil and criminal investigations related to this incident;

5. Expresses grave concern at reports of insufficient and limited access to the crash site;

6. Demands that the armed groups in control of the crash site and the surrounding area refrain from any actions that may compromise the integrity of the crash site, including by refraining from destroying, moving, or disturbing wreckage, equipment, debris, personal belongings,

or remains, and immediately provide safe, secure, full and unrestricted access to the site and surrounding area for the appropriate investigating authorities, the OSCE Special Monitoring Mission and representatives of other relevant international organizations according to ICAO and other established procedures;

7. Demands that all military activities, including by armed groups, be immediately ceased in the immediate area surrounding the crash site to allow for security and safety of the international investigation;

8. Insists on the dignified, respectful and professional treatment and recovery of the bodies of the victims, and calls upon all parties to ensure that this happens with immediate effect;

9. Calls on all States and actors in the region to cooperate fully in relation to the international investigation of the incident, including with respect to immediate and unrestricted access to the crash site as referred to in paragraph 6;

10. Welcomes in this regard the statement on 17 July 2014 by the Trilateral Contact Group of senior representatives of Ukraine, the Russian Federation and the OSCE and demands that the commitments outlined in that statement be implemented in full;

11. Demands that those responsible for this incident be held to account and that all States cooperate fully with efforts to establish accountability;

12. Urges all parties to the Convention on International Civil Aviation to observe to the fullest extent applicable, the international rules, standards and practices concerning the safety of civil aviation, in order to prevent the recurrence of such incidents, and demands that all States and other actors refrain from acts of violence directed against civilian aircraft;

13. Welcomes the full cooperation of the United Nations offered by the Secretary-General in this investigation, and requests the Secretary-General to identify possible options for United Nations support to the investigation and to report to the Security Council on relevant developments;

14. Decides to remain seized of the matter.

Milestones and mourning

As anyone who has experienced loss will understand, the usual milestones become harder to face without your loved ones there. Birthdays, anniversaries, holidays, the dates on the calendar you once looked forward to now arrive with a sharp edge, a reminder of who is missing. They seem to come around quickly, and they are plentiful.

Just eight days after MH17, we held Sophie's birthday party at our house. In some ways, it felt impossible to celebrate anything so soon after losing Mum and Dad. But children don't measure time the way adults do, and in keeping with maintaining as much normality as possible for the kids, the party went ahead, minus two people. Sophie was still young enough for birthdays to mean a party with balloons, a cake with candles and, of course, presents. We wanted her to feel the joy she deserved. So, we put up decorations, tidied the house and welcomed people in. On the surface, it probably looked like any other birthday gathering. But beneath it all, there was a weight in the air. A sense of going through the motions because life demanded it, because children remind us to keep moving forward, even when our hearts aren't ready.

Mum and Dad would have been there; they loved nothing more than to celebrate the birthdays of their grandchildren. In fact, they had planned their overseas travel so that they would be back in plenty of time to make it to their granddaughter's birthday. They would have helped set up the party, brought a card and a present, stood in the background, taking photos, smiling as Sophie blew out her candles. Their absence that day was loud in its silence. It hung around the edges of the celebration, a grief we carried quietly so that Sophie didn't have to.

It's an absence that Sophie has carried with her every year when her birthday comes around. It's hard not to; her birthday will always be within that week of the passing of her grandparents. Birthdays are meant to be milestones to celebrate, but for Sophie, it will always be another painful reminder of what happened.

At Sophie's birthday party, something unexpected happened. It was something small, but it stayed with me. Among the guests was someone who hadn't yet heard about the fate of my parents, or at least they hadn't connected the dots. They arrived, chatted, laughed, asked how we were, just as they normally would. For a little while, we spoke as if nothing had happened. No awkward silences, no sad glances, no heavy questions hanging between us. Just a normal conversation about normal things. Days later, he realised what had happened and apologised. There was no apology necessary; from my perspective, it was all fine. He did wonder why we had so many flowers in the house and then it all started to make sense for him.

It might sound strange, but in that moment, it was a relief. Grief had become this weight I carried everywhere, shaping every interaction, every conversation. To speak to someone, even briefly, who didn't know, who wasn't tiptoeing around the tragedy, felt like stepping out from under a shadow. For those few minutes, I could just be myself. Not the grieving son, not the victim of something horrific. Just Matthew, talking about everyday things.

It reminded me how important those small, ordinary connections are. How sometimes what we need most is not sympathy or solemnity, but simply a moment of lightness, a reminder that life, even in its darkest moments, still contains space for the ordinary, the human and the kind. It was an early reminder that supporting someone through grief can be as simple as treating them like you always did.

I mentioned earlier how important it felt to me to try and maintain some sense of normality for the kids. Amid the grief, the uncertainty and the public nature of what had happened, I wanted them to keep going – school, activities, friends, the routines that grounded them. For the most part, we managed to hold onto that. The school parent community rallied around us. Word spread quickly and people wanted to help. They wanted to do something practical, something tangible. One of the most thoughtful gestures came in the form of a simple solution – meals, namely dinner, every night.

Each afternoon when we picked up the kids from school, we would also pick up a home-cooked meal prepared by another family. They put themselves on a roster, purposefully and efficiently, and for three weeks, we came home each night to food we didn't have to think about. In those days when even getting out of bed took energy, when decisions felt impossibly hard, and everything seemed heavier than it should be, having a hot meal ready to go was more than kindness; it was relief. It was one less thing to worry about.

Somewhere along the line, it seemed that every third meal we received was lasagne. I started to joke that there must have been a secret lasagne committee operating behind the scenes, determined to see us through with layers of pasta, sauce and cheese. They were all different and delicious. Ironically, our mum made the best lasagne you have ever tasted, and none of the lasagnes we had came close to Mum's cooking. But truthfully, every meal, whether it was lasagne or something else, carried with it more than just food. It carried care. It carried love. It carried an important message: 'You're not alone. We're thinking of you. We want to help..

In those weeks, that mattered more than anyone probably realised. And no doubt it helped keep us together and get us ready for the memorial events we were about to embark on.

On August 7, 2014, around three weeks after the downing, Australia paused for a National Day of Mourning to honour the thirty-eight Australian citizens and residents who were killed when Flight MH17 was shot down. A National Memorial Service was held on the same day at St Patrick's Cathedral in Melbourne, and through the support of the Australian Government, we were able to travel to Melbourne for the

The National Day of Mourning in Melbourne

service. It was a solemn and dignified setting for a tragedy that had left families shattered and a nation grieving. Flags across the country flew at half-mast. A minute's silence was observed. For one day, the noise of politics and news cycles seemed to quiet, replaced by something simpler and more human – remembrance.

Leaders were in attendance, including Governor-General Sir Peter Cosgrove, who had also called us in those first few days. The Governor-General reinforced Australia's position to bring back our parents and ensure a thorough investigation take place. Other attendees included Prime Minister Tony Abbott, Foreign Affairs Minister Julie Bishop, opposition figures, state premiers, diplomats and community representatives. But the day was not about politics. It was about families. It was about acknowledging lives lost far too soon and publicly recognising the private devastation carried by those left behind.

The service was multi-faith, reflecting the diversity of the victims and their families. Words were spoken about grief, resilience, love and hope, but there was no attempt to dress up the pain or offer hollow comforts. It was a day to simply stand still and mourn. Part of the service included the reading of the names of all the victims. It is never easy to hear your parents' names in those circumstances, and equally not easy to hear all the other names as well.

Following the service, there was a reception across the road from the cathedral in a hotel function room. I remember the day well, considering how much of a blur things were at the time. I remember chatting to the Prime Minister and meeting him face to face. Tony introduced himself and we got talking. He inquired again about my parents and seemed genuinely interested in them. What was simply amazing, though, was that he remembered in detail all the things we had talked about over the phone a few weeks earlier. His recall was incredible and showed that he listened. I have no doubt that he had some good notes and a briefing prior to the event, but I watched him work the room and saw that he had the same genuine interest in all he spoke to. It reaffirmed to me that the Prime Minister was genuine in his resolve to help the families, bring home the deceased Australians and provide the leadership needed for a proper investigation.

It was also the day we met Julie Bishop in person for the first time. Again, Julie was firm in her commitment to the families and genuinely interested in our wellbeing and supporting us in any way possible. Julie wasn't just a politician; she was incredibly passionate about doing a good job and doing it right.

Another memorable moment was a performance from Australian artist Katie Noonan. Katie performed a couple of songs during the service, but the one that stood out for me was *Even When I'm Sleeping* by Leonardo's Bride. Katie sang the song with Abby Dobson, and for me, it was the perfect song for the occasion. Words from the chorus include, 'When I close my eyes, you're everywhere.'

This is very much how it felt during those first few months; I felt like I could see and hear my parents everywhere. Music gets you sometimes, and whenever I hear that song, it takes me back to that memorial service, and I think about my parents. Ten years later, I met Katie in Caloundra while she was on tour in 2024. I was able to chat with her about the MH17 memorial service and thank her for the memories she helped create with that performance.

For families like mine, the National Day of Mourning and the service offered a strange comfort that I had not experienced previously. Nothing could undo what had been done. Nothing could bring our loved ones home. But to see the nation pause, to hear the names spoken aloud in such a public space, was to know that we were not alone in our grief. It didn't lessen the pain, but gave it shape. It gave us a place to stand and a moment to breathe. In the grand cathedral and across the country, we knew that Australia was with us, and possibly for the first time I understood why a service like that it important to the families of the victims.

It was also the first time I had seen grief on a larger scale. There were hundreds of affected family members from across Australia at the service; all of us had the same thing happen to us and we were all affected by the same event, but everyone was grieving in different ways. There were family members who were inconsolable, unable to control themselves physically. The pain and sadness were there for all to see. For others, it was almost as if nothing had happened, taking photos, chatting to people like just another day. Grief and sadness hits everyone differently.

At the time of the National Day of Mourning, we had no idea if we would ever get Mum and Dad back. No one could give us those answers. The advice we received was deliberately broad and cautious – retrieval, identification and repatriation could take months or might never happen at all. There was no guarantee that we would receive a body or a body part. In the cloud of uncertainty, planning something like a funeral felt impossible. How do you plan to say goodbye when you don't even know if you'll have the chance?

Our family made the decision to organise a memorial service. A celebration of life. It was held on August 15, 2014, in the Grand Ballroom at Eatons Hill Hotel in Brisbane. In a way, it became something tangible to focus on in a time when everything else felt completely beyond our control. We poured ourselves into it – big screens, audio-visuals, photos, music, seating plans, speeches. It was a production in every sense, but it was also something more. It gave us purpose in the void. It brought focus to days that otherwise blurred together. It was everything you would do for a funeral, maybe more.

The generosity of everyone was incredible. The hotel offered the ballroom for free, and all production costs were significantly discounted. We prepared video montages with photos set to music, and each of us had our own speech. David provided us with some laughable moments when he got his speech pages out of order and he got totally lost. It didn't matter, but it was funny, and the lesson learnt was to number your pages.

We even had memorial pins with a sunflower photo and Howard and Susan written on them. They were made for us for free, but rather than hand them out, we sold them for $5 a pin. All the funds raised were donated to Mum and Dad's preferred charity, the Cancer Council Queensland. More than $2500 was raised that day.

More than 700 people attended. Family, friends, colleagues, neighbours, people whose lives had been touched by Mum and Dad in ways we hadn't even known. Politicians from federal, state and local government came, and a letter from the Prime Minister was read out as part of the proceedings. Mirusia Louwerse, an Australian soprano who had been touring with André Rieu at the time, attended and gave a lovely speech for Mum and Dad. Mum and Dad's siblings and good friends of my parents, and, of course, the three of us all spoke. With such a big crowd, it was daunting, but also easy; there really were no wrong words.

In the room that day, conducting a production we didn't ask for and hearing the words spoken, seeing so many family and friends gathered, I realised this was probably the first thing we had done that contributed to our healing. Not closure, not yet, not even close. But healing. A way to honour Mum and Dad in the absence of certainty, to acknowledge the grief, to share it with others, to feel less alone. It provided a chance for so many mourners to also start to say goodbye. So many people were waiting for answers, not just our family.

Looking back, I'm not entirely sure how we found the strength to pull it all together. Nor do I know how we managed it in such a professional way. Grief steals so much energy, and yet somehow, this gave us something back. It gave us a moment to say, 'They mattered. They are loved. And we will carry them forward.'

I remember Grandpa coming up to me after the service; he had lost his daughter and son-in-law. I gave him the opportunity to speak and be part of the service, but he was too distraught to do so. He told me how incredibly proud he was of the three of us. He said it was a credit to Mum and Dad and to us how well we spoke and how well organised it was. Even in his grief, he could see good things. Grandpa was always good like that. I can't imagine how he felt sitting in the crowd watching that service. Just horrible for a dad to live through.

In the lead-up to the service, I had spent considerable time seeking out someone who would be happy to emcee for us. This became incredibly difficult as every time I asked someone, they said they couldn't do it because they were too emotional. In hindsight, I understand. The people I was asking were connected to Mum and Dad in some way. But at the time, I couldn't understand why I was getting so many knockbacks. *Surely there is no one more emotional than me?*

I asked fifteen different people and got the same response. I resigned and prepared to do it myself. Then, a couple of days before, I received a call from someone who said they might be able to help. It was a work colleague of a friend of one of Dad's friends. I was provided a contact name and a phone number, as he was not someone known to me. I was feeling desperate at that stage, so I rang the number.

The person was Paul Reis, and we agreed to meet the next day, which was the day before the service. I sat down for a coffee with Paul and immediately had a sense that this was the guy for us. At the time, Paul worked with the Mater Foundation and was a qualified celebrant, having done numerous weddings and some funerals. In a former role, Paul was based in Tasmania and had done many of the funeral services for the victims of the Port Arthur massacre back in 1996. The massacre was the worst mass shooting in Australia and a headline story for such a long time. While it was different to our circumstances, there were so many similarities. It dawned on me that Paul was experienced with this type of tragedy and was perfect for our needs. I could hardly believe it. I gave Paul the emcee notes that I had prepared for myself and he ran the service for us the next day. It was such a weight off my shoulders. Paul and I have been friends ever since.

Amsterdam

Amsterdam will always be connected to MH17. It was from Amsterdam's Schiphol Airport, one of Europe's busiest and most well-known airports, that flight MH17 departed on July 17, 2014, bound for Kuala Lumpur. For many families, including ours, Amsterdam became an unexpected and central part of our story.

What should have been just another ordinary departure became the starting point of an international tragedy. In the months that followed, Amsterdam, the Netherlands, and its people played a significant role in the repatriation, investigation and care of those lost. It became a place not just of transit, but of remembrance, of ceremony and of grief. For us, returning to Amsterdam over the last ten years has been about more than visiting a city; it has been about reconnecting with the place where our parents' final journey began and finding ways to honour them in a city that, in its quiet way, has become part of our family's history.

The Australian Government's actions on the ground in Ukraine and the Netherlands were swift, determined and deeply focused on ensuring justice, dignity and support for the families affected. It followed

Amsterdam, a second home

on from the leadership and direction provided by Tony Abbott and Julie Bishop. While it's impossible to capture every detail of such a complex international effort, what stands out most to me is the commitment Australia showed to doing the right thing, not just for its own citizens, but in helping to uphold standards of respect and accountability for everyone on board that flight. At various times throughout the repatriation and investigation, several hundred Australian personnel were deployed to work on the case. Much of this work and support was not readily known to us at the time but certainly became a feature.

From the earliest days, Australia played a leading role in the international response. Through diplomatic channels, intelligence sharing and the strength of its relationships with the Netherlands and Ukraine, Australia worked tirelessly to secure access to the crash site in what was then, and still is, an active conflict zone in an incredibly unstable environment. This was no simple task as the separatist group (backed by

Russia) and Ukrainian armed forces battled away all through the crash site. The AFP and DFAT officials were almost immediately deployed to Europe to support this mission, working alongside their Dutch and Malaysian counterparts as part of the Joint Investigation Team (JIT). The first staff arrived within four days of the plane going down. Their aim was clear: to recover the remains with dignity, secure evidence and ensure a thorough investigation could proceed.

In Ukraine, where access was initially blocked by armed separatists, Australia pushed diplomatically and through the adoption of Resolution 2166, which demanded access to the crash site to recover human remains and for a full investigation. On the ground, AFP officers were deployed as part of Operation Bring Them Home, a mission that saw Australian police and forensic specialists working in difficult and dangerous conditions to locate and retrieve remains and personal effects. Their work was marked by both precision and compassion, recognising the enormous weight of their task. A task made more difficult as the Russian Federation provided no support to the recovery efforts or investigation.

In the Netherlands, Australia established a strong presence to support the identification and repatriation process. AFP forensic teams worked alongside Dutch authorities at Hilversum Military Base, painstakingly undertaking the complex process of DNA matching and identification. Incredibly, we learned that Australia is a leader in this type of identification; we have experience with notable examples, including the victim identification for the Bali Bombings and the Boxing Day Tsunami near Banda Aceh. Australia's officials ensured that families were kept informed and that the process was carried out with the utmost care and respect. The collaboration between Australian, Dutch and other international teams was a model of professionalism in the face of tragedy.

Australia's efforts extended beyond the immediate crisis. The government advocated strongly for accountability, supporting the ongoing criminal investigations and legal processes through the JIT. This wasn't just about securing justice for Australian families; it was about upholding international law and challenging the impunity of those responsible.

What Australia did, diligently, with determination and compassion, mattered. It mattered to the families. It mattered to the broader cause of justice. And it demonstrated that even in the face of senseless tragedy, governments can act with purpose, humanity and courage. Most of all, the support has continued through the decade for our family, from the repatriation to all the legal proceedings.

For what seemed like a long time, we had no real thought that we would get our parents back. For days and weeks, we saw footage of crews on the ground conducting recovery exercises and seeing body bags and caskets being returned to the Netherlands for identification. The bodies and body parts were collected from the various locations in the crash site and placed together for collection. They sat in the sun and elements for days before they were transported by train – known as the 'train of death' – from Torez (now Chystiakove) to Kharkiv. Body bags after body bags were placed into refrigerated carriages for the trip.

We now know that Mum and Dad were in those body bags, but at the time, we didn't, and we had no way of knowing anything. We didn't know who picked them up, exactly where they were collected or whether they had even been collected in the first place. The investigation site, at more than fifty square kilometres in size, was dubbed one of the largest in the world. In Kharkiv, the bodies were handed to Dutch and Australian authorities, where they were flown back to the Netherlands, to Eindhoven airport, and onto Hilversum for identification. Once in the Netherlands, the bodies were treated with the utmost respect and care; things had changed from the horror of the crash site in Ukraine amidst a brewing conflict and the harsh elements of a Ukrainian summer.

We did our part to support the identification process by providing DNA samples. The whole process was unsurprisingly new to us. Of course, you often hear about DNA, whether in the media or in a TV show or similar. However, I had never been exposed to DNA, and I had never been asked to provide a sample. Of course, that all changed with what we have been through, and it was an important step in the identification of our parents' bodies. We each provided saliva swabs and hair samples. An extensive questionnaire had to be completed. We were asked everything we knew about body features, eye and hair colour, tattoos. Anything and everything that could help. Recent photos were also provided. David again provided the humour; his ability to recall all the features of our parents was remarkable, including making a point of telling the police that Dad was circumcised, which might help with the identification. I'm not sure if it mattered, but they wrote down the details.

As usual, the AFP was looking out for us. In taking the samples, the AFP enlisted the Queensland Police Service rather than taking them through the federal police. This was done to cover us off for any future use of the sample, say through the State Coroner, for example. The federal legislation didn't allow state governments to access the files; however, the state legislation allowed the federal agencies to access the data. So, put simply, we only needed to provide one sample and complete one set of documentation. Not only did this improve efficiency, but it also supported families during a difficult and emotional time. Other medical and dental records were also accessed to support the identification process.

In supporting the identification process, we knew that it could be a long road ahead in terms of having a successful identification. However, on the night of the memorial service that we held for our parents, I received a call from our AFP contact. It was a Friday night, and it was getting late, around nine. Nonetheless, I took the call. It had been a big day, and it was about to get bigger. Authorities in the Netherlands had identified

Mum. Four weeks after her death, it was the news we had been waiting for. It would have almost been exciting if it weren't so tragic. However, that relief was short-lived as they still had not identified Dad. We, of course, asked about Dad but they had no answers.

Logistically, the AFP wanted to start the repatriation for Mum. We were asked about what we wanted to do about bringing her back; they had pre-arranged repatriation flights in anticipation of positive identifications. But we didn't want to bring Mum back without Dad, so we decided to wait for as long as was possible in the hope that we could bring them home together. To us, it was logical that Mum and Dad would have fallen to their death together as they were seated next to each other, so surely they were transported to the Netherlands somewhat together. But your mind can start to play tricks on you and different scenarios run through your head.

What if one of them was in the toilet or had gone for a walk on the plane to stretch their legs? We will never know, but it's hard not to think about it, especially when you are waiting for answers.

We didn't have to wait long. Five days after receiving the news about Mum, we received a similar phone call, this time to say that Dad had been identified. Mind you, five days felt like a lifetime. It is hard to describe the feeling at the time as we had confirmation that both of our parents were dead, but we also now had the chance to bring them home together. They left on the trip together; they died together and now they could come home together. Everything in those couple of days felt like it was happening quickly. The AFP and DFAT were amazing. There was a planned repatriation scheduled for a couple of weeks' time, on September 9, 2014, so we agreed to be ready for it.

It was a huge comfort to know that these things were being organised for us. I could never imagine trying to organise such an exercise without any support. The proposal was to fly us over a day or two beforehand, be part of a private service in Amsterdam before joining other families in Eindhoven for a ramp ceremony to load the bodies onto a plane. We would then be flown back to Melbourne in time to meet other family members for a ramp ceremony at the other end.

David had left London in such a hurry that he had no chance to really consider his affairs before leaving. In those few weeks back home, he had decided to move back to Australia, so it made sense to try to get to London and pack David up on this trip. DFAT was helpful with this request, and within days of confirming the identity of both our parents, on August 25, 2014, the three of us flew to London. This was my first long-haul flight since Mum and Dad's death, and I was nervous and apprehensive. As someone who loves travel, this was an uneasy time. I remember telling myself that flying was safe, but on that flight, all I could think about was my parents. I still do, every time I fly.

The time in London was tough; going through David's belongings from the past thirteen years was never going to be easy, and having to do it under such difficult circumstances made it more emotional. The trip was also healing. We experienced many of the places and things that Mum and Dad did with David when they had visited him in July of that year. We almost escaped the noise of MH17 at home. London was a big city and just kept moving like it always did. The escape was needed, even if we didn't intend it in that way.

On September 6, 2014, a couple of weeks after arriving in London, we flew across to Amsterdam for the repatriation. We met up with other families who had just flown in from Australia. They were exhausted and weary. As we had been in London, I felt much fresher and was almost ready for what I was about to face in Amsterdam. I say *almost*, because I tended to underestimate the emotional and physical impacts of these events. When you've never experienced anything like it before, how can you really prepare?

The first day or so in Amsterdam was low-key; we had time to ourselves and used it to retrace some of Mum and Dad's last steps and to enjoy some of what Amsterdam has to offer. Seeing the sights and experiencing the culture that Mum and Dad had enjoyed only months earlier was surprisingly healing. I remember we stayed at a Holiday Inn Express, which was away from the city centre, but nothing was too far on a bike in Amsterdam. The hotel had bikes we could use, so off we went, riding up to the beautiful Vondelpark and into town.

Following our parents' steps was easier said than done, as the streets and canals in Amsterdam tend to blend into one, especially if you are not familiar with the area. All we had to go on were photos from Dad's Facebook posts. We were fortunate that he had posted regularly, so we had some idea of where they went.

There was one place where there was a photo of Mum and a delicious looking serving of strawberry pancakes with ice cream. The photo didn't give away much. It showed the inside of the restaurant, so you could get a look and feel, but it didn't show the outside, nor was there a name. So, finding this place was like finding a needle in a haystack. There were other photos from that day on Dad's Facebook, so we wandered and walked around the same streets, just as Mum and Dad had done during their visit.

And then, on one of the busier streets in Amsterdam, we found it – Petit Restaurant, De Rozenboom. Billed as an original Dutch restaurant, the food pays homage to the spirit of true Dutch fare. The interior is creative, decorated with Delft blue plates and wooden tables and chairs, giving it a rustic Dutch look. Once inside, it was clear this was the place Mum and Dad had been. We were able to sit at the same table and order the exact same strawberry pancakes. It could have been a sad moment, but there was something quite healing about finding this place and doing as Mum and Dad did. Another example of them guiding us and almost telling us what to do and how to enjoy Amsterdam.

Sitting at the table, I looked up at the wall, which was covered with all the Delft blue plates. The plate closest to me read:

'If everything seems to be going well, you obviously don't know what the hell is going on.'

It wasn't meant for me, I'm sure. Just a joke on a plate in a Dutch restaurant. But in that moment, it felt like the universe was winking darkly in my direction. Maybe even Mum was winking at me, as she often had a saying for everything. Because at the time, nothing seemed to be going well. Beneath the surface, I knew exactly what was going on, and it was unbearable. That small, unexpected sign became one of those odd details that lodges itself in your memory, not for its wisdom, but for its timing. A reminder that even grief comes with moments of absurdity, and that the world keeps spinning, indifferent to whether we understand it.

It was on September 8, 2014, at a funeral home at Westgaarde, not far from Schiphol Airport, that we were finally reunited with our parents. DFAT had arranged for transport, and we were greeted at the hotel by a black Mercedes van with dark-tinted windscreens. Think CIA-type operation. We had our own driver who opened the door for us, gave us water and did whatever we asked of them. In we hopped and off we went on the twenty-minute drive.

There had been quite a buildup to that point, but maybe because we had been in London, I was partially in holiday mode. Logically, I knew we were about to be reunited with Mum and Dad, except they were in caskets. The confronting reality hit me hard. We were asked to stand at the end of a long, tree-lined road, and you could see two hearses turn on to the road at the other end, directly ahead of us. The drive down the roadside towards us seemed to take forever because they were driving at walking pace. It was probably what you would expect for this kind of service, but it seems to prolong the process. As they got closer, and I could see the caskets in the back, I cried. That is all I remember about that moment. I'm not sure how you would describe it, but it was a deep, painful cry. I had cried in the days and weeks prior, but this was different; after weeks and days of waiting, confirmation that we weren't getting them back, perhaps and a huge reality check. The grief was on full show at that moment as it poured out.

Once the hearses drove down the road and past us, they parked behind the main building. We were taken inside to a small funeral room. The room had two parts, one had the doors shut and outside that room was an area that had food, drinks and a coffee machine. Nothing fancy, but enough food for twenty people, and there were only the three of us. It was at that moment that I realised we were having our own funeral service for Mum and Dad. It was probably explained to us, but it never really clicked until we got there. The innocence of it all was nice, but I kind of wished I were more prepared. I grabbed a drink and was greeted by the funeral celebrant. 'We are ready for you now.'

The closed doors opened, and inside that room were Mum and Dad's caskets, the two of them side by side in a V shape. The three of us went in and they shut the door behind us. It was our family, the five of us together. Our lives had been torn apart in those last six weeks, but somehow, we were together again.

I don't think any of us really knew what to do. Outside the room, we were asked if we wanted any music played. We had picked some André Rieu, probably because that might have been what Mum and Dad wanted, so it was playing in the background. I think we decided to say something, so I started talking. It was odd, I can't remember the exact words, but I told Mum and Dad that we missed them and that people were looking after us. Some of it sounded weird and silly, and we started laughing at each other because we were talking to two dead people. There are no rules, but it was surreal. We took photos. Why? I don't know. When I look back at those photos, you can see us trying to smile. We always seemed to be smiling in these photos. Selfies with Mum and Dad's caskets. In hindsight, the photos are good to look back on to reflect what we have been through. But I still don't know what compelled us to take photos, or why we were smiling. I guess we are always told to smile in photos and that instinct kicked in.

We decided to take turns spending time alone with Mum and Dad. As my brothers left the room, I said a few more words, told my parents about their grandkids, what they were up to and how much they missed them. I cried again; it was such a sad moment. It was also possibly the first time I really realised the impact of their loss on my kids. Just terrible. I took more photos, another selfie, I don't know why. I decided I'd had enough and let one of the others in. I went outside and tried to eat, but I just didn't feel like it.

After each of my brothers had some alone time with Mum and Dad, we said our goodbyes and made our way back to the accommodation. The black Mercedes was waiting for us. I am pretty sure these cars only get used by celebrities, politicians and other VIPs. We were getting the VIP treatment, but it was a quiet trip back to the hotel.

Bringing them home

One of the highlights while visiting Amsterdam was a small, much-loved restaurant called Moeders, the Dutch word for 'mothers'. Mum and Dad enjoyed visiting Moeders and it was one of their favourite places to eat. It's not a grand place by any stretch, but that's precisely its charm. The walls are crowded with photographs, hundreds, maybe thousands, of mothers from across the world. Smiling, posed, sometimes faded with time, they form a collage of love and lineage that wraps itself around the room like a warm embrace. Every inch of the space feels like a tribute to family, to tradition, to the strength of the people who so often hold households together.

Moeders serves hearty, traditional Dutch comfort food, just as a Dutch mum would serve up – stamppot, bitterballen, stews that arrive steaming and rich, meals designed to fill not just the stomach but something deeper. It also has a pretty good apple pie, which is often sold out. It's the sort of place where you quickly feel like a local and where the food isn't trying to impress, it's simply trying to comfort, to remind you of home, even if you're far from it. The restaurant is busy enough to require booking in advance.

My first visit to Moeders was on September 6, 2014, on the repatriation trip to Amsterdam. We had known the restaurant was a favourite place of Mum and Dad's, and introduced ourselves to the owner Jurriaan van der Reijden, who founded it back in 1990 and continues to run it today. He's the creative force behind its warm, nostalgic concept. Jurriaan's guiding vision for Moeders was clear from the start: to recreate that sense of home so many people might be missing, especially their mothers. At the grand opening, he invited guests to bring their own plate, glass or cutlery, which could be left behind, weaving together a table that felt shared and familiar. That eclectic mix of vintage tableware still graces the wooden tables, adding to the unique vibe. Nothing matches, just as you might expect when you visit your mum or grandmother's place.

Jurriaan also asked those first guests to bring a photo of their mum to put on the wall. When we arrived for our first visit, the walls were full. Every spare space had been used and then some. We had a photo of our mum, hoping that we might be able to put it up. Jurriaan was great and made space for the photo. He even had a spare photo frame for Mum's photo. However, in the process, he took another photo off the wall to make room. You could almost hear the gasping of the other patrons in the restaurant at the time – that was someone's mum. He assured us that it was okay to be taking down the photo; he seemed to know every photo and every story in the room. It was his restaurant after all.

It was a very special moment, and now Moeders holds a special place in our hearts. Once the photo was on the wall, Jurriaan came over to our table with a bottle of Schylger Jutters-Bitter, a herbal bitter from his home, Terschelling, one of the small islands in the north of the Netherlands. It is a tasty, bitter drink made from herbs that have grown in the dunes of Terschelling since ancient times. This bitter contains thirty

Moeders. Susan's photo is on this wall twice.

per cent alcohol. It was served to us cold and in a shot glass, and we were encouraged to drink it in a similar way to drinking a shot. Jurriaan invited all the staff who were working to join us at our table and poured each of them a shot to have a toast to our mum, who was now on the wall, and Dad. It was a beautiful way to honour our parents and to hear Jurriaan talk about his hometown. We have been back to Moeders multiple times, and every time we go, Jurriaan pours us a shot of Schylger Jutters-Bitters and has a toast for Mum and Dad. Even the kids got a shot when we visited in 2023, a great story for them to share with their mates.

Moeders is more than just a restaurant to us. It's a reminder that no matter where you go, love, family and home-cooked meals will always find a way to follow. Moeders provides that home comfort when you are away from home.

The repatriation flight had been organised for the next day, which was also when we were due to fly out of Amsterdam for Melbourne. It was another big, hectic day. The repatriation flight was taking place out of Eindhoven Airport, a ninety-minute drive from Amsterdam. The airport is used by both civilian and military aircraft. Mum and Dad had flown into Eindhoven on previous travels to the Netherlands. The repatriation would take place with other families – there were five families in total. This meant five black Mercedes vans, one for each family. We were packed up with our luggage, ready to travel home to Australia. We hopped in and were whisked away, literally. It felt like the drivers were trying to break some sort of record to get to Eindhoven. We drove in formation, following each other closely at high speed. None of us was sure what was going on, but we felt like we were in a Bond movie; I'm just not sure who the villain was. David asked if they could slow down a bit, but we got told we were driving in convoy.

Mum and Dad were on the second repatriation flight organised by the Royal Australian Air Force (RAAF). They travelled on a Boeing C-17 Globemaster. The RAAF had several of these aircraft, which have a high capacity to perform a range of tasks, both in wartime and peacekeeping. They are based in Queensland at the Amberley base. On this day, they were taking Mum and Dad home, along with seven other victims. The aircraft's serial number was A41-210, and the plane was parked on the airport apron, just outside one of the terminals, away from the civilian part of the airport. On the apron were about twenty empty chairs. We were taken inside the terminal for a short reception. The authorities there explained what was going to happen and there was food and drinks. I don't think I ate anything, but there was never an excuse for being hungry.

After a while, we were led down to the tarmac to sit in the chairs. I remember sitting down with my brothers on one side of me and a woman on the other. Her name was Michelle Lee and she was the daughter of two victims. This was the first time we had met, and Michelle started chatting to me, which broke the ice, so to speak. I can't remember what we chatted about, but I'm grateful it seemed to ease the tension. We learnt quickly that we were both there for our respective parents. We didn't have long to chat as the ceremony started. From our left, nine hearses arrived, carrying one body each. The hearses drove slowly onto the tarmac, just as they did at Westgaarde, and made their way past all the family members before turning to line up in formation behind the waiting C-17. The rear door of the C-17 was open, ready to receive its cargo.

The Dutch authorities, military and funeral services showed remarkable respect in how they approached these deeply sensitive moments. The loading ceremony itself was precise and choreographed to perfection. At the airfield, each coffin was draped with the Australian flag and carried with care by members of the Dutch military. Five separate loadings, one for each family, which meant Mum and Dad were loaded together. The ceremony was marked by silence, apart from the measured steps of the pallbearers and the sound of the aircraft waiting in the distance. Every movement seemed to acknowledge the weight of what was being carried, not just in physical terms but also emotionally and symbolically. It wasn't simply a logistical process; it was a final act of honour as those nine family members started their second attempt to travel home.

Seeing Mum and Dad included in that moment, carried by strangers who nonetheless seemed to understand the enormity of their task, gave me

Boarding in Eindhoven
to return to Australia

Not the way you are supposed to come home

a small sense of peace. They were leaving Europe in the most respectful, dignified way possible. All nine bodies were loaded into the back of the C-17 and the rear door was closed.

Before long, all family members were back in the five Mercedes making our way to Schiphol Airport in Amsterdam to board our flight home. The timing was tight and so the trip back to Amsterdam felt like it had on the way out there. Fast, in convoy and in formation. We were dropped off at the airport and fast-tracked through check-in and customs. We boarded our flight and started to make our way to Melbourne; the goal was to be back in Melbourne in time to see the C-17 unloaded.

Around twenty-four hours later, we arrived in Melbourne, where we were greeted by our family members. Holly was there along with Mum and Dad's siblings. DFAT had arranged for the additional family members to be on hand for the unloading of the C-17. We arrived in the evening and were booked into a hotel overnight, ready for the ceremony the next morning, which was held at one of the smaller remote hangars at

Melbourne airport. We were driven out to the hangar in a bus. One of the things I remember was the line of photographers on the way out; they had been prevented from being near the hangar but were still hoping for a photo of us. They were out of luck, but it sticks in my mind that they even tried. Once we arrived at the hangar, we were taken inside, where nine hearses were ready to receive a casket each. The large hangar door was open with the C-17 outside backed up to the hangar. The ceremony commenced with the rear door of the C-17 opening, which was the only thing you could hear in the silence. It was loud.

Then the bagpipes started playing. Nothing gets the emotions going more than bagpipes at a solemn service, such as a ramp ceremony. Just as they were in Eindhoven, the bodies were carried off the aircraft, only this time, in reverse order. They were carried by Australian servicemen and women and placed on the trolleys at the back of each hearse. Once all the bodies were removed, family members were able to go over to the caskets to pay their respects. In our case, Mum and Dad were nearly home, but

Treated with the most respect on their final journey

the journey was not quite done yet. The caskets were loaded into the cars and driven off past the waiting paparazzi towards the Victorian Coroner.

Tony Abbott had said he would bring them home, and he did. We made our way back to the domestic terminal, where we travelled to Brisbane after an exhausting trip.

I arrived home, and one of the items in the mail was a letter from Clarence House, from Prince Charles, offering his deepest sympathy. I opened the letter, unsure at first who it was from. In the end, I googled the signature to work out it was Prince Charles. It was somewhat odd, yet another reminder of the moments we were experiencing. I am not sure why the Royal family was writing to us, but in some ways, it helped make a difference. Notably, they spelled Mum's name wrong – Suzanne?

The bodies of all Australian victims arrived in Melbourne so they could be formally received and processed under the guidance of the Victorian Coroner. This step, clinical though it may seem, was handled with deep sensitivity. Every official involved understood the weight of their task and that these were not just remains, but people cherished and mourned by their families. The process was painstaking but necessary, ensuring accuracy, dignity and respect at every turn and included an inquest into the deaths of the Victorians who lost their lives.

Once the formalities in Melbourne were complete, Mum and Dad were flown home to Queensland on a Qantas flight. Even that small detail, flying Qantas, seemed to bring a familiar comfort. It felt right, familiar, Australian. There was no fanfare, no formality, just a flight home. Their final journey home was no less significant for its simplicity. It was about closing a circle, bringing them back to the place where they had lived, loved and raised their family. We received a phone call from our funeral director, who had picked up the caskets from the airport and had them in their morgue. We could now organise the funeral.

Mum and Dad were finally home.

Following the repatriation, we had always said we needed to visit Amsterdam and the Netherlands again, in happier times, so that we could truly enjoy what the Dutch have to offer.

In 2015, we travelled to Europe for the annual André Rieu concerts in Maastricht. The trip came about through an invitation from some of Mum and Dad's friends, who had helped organise tickets and wanted to share this experience with us. It felt like the right time to go, to show the kids a part of the world their grandparents had loved, to keep moving forward, and to find small moments of joy again. We travelled through Rome, Florence, Venice, Zurich, Freiburg (where we had Black Forest cake in the actual Black Forest, as you do), Heidelberg and finally Amsterdam before making our way to Maastricht.

When we arrived in Amsterdam, I had carefully chosen a hotel: Hotel Amsterdam De Roode Leeuw. I believed this was the place Mum and Dad had stayed on their last visit. There was something comforting in that, the idea of walking the same hallways, staying under the same roof, feeling close to them in a city where they'd once been happy. When we checked in, I shared our story with the staff. They were so kind. I asked if they could find any record of Mum and Dad's stay and perhaps tell us which room they'd been in. They promised to investigate it.

Days passed and we didn't hear back. Towards the end of our stay, one of the staff approached us, apologetic and gentle. They couldn't find any record of Mum and Dad ever staying there. They were genuinely sorry and so was I. I thanked them for trying. It wasn't until we returned home and I went through some of Mum and Dad's papers that I realised we had stayed at the wrong hotel. Mum and Dad had been somewhere else entirely.

At first, I felt a wave of embarrassment. All that fuss over the wrong place. But almost immediately after, I felt some relief. It was another reminder that grief can cloud your thinking. I was certain we booked the same hotel, however, there was another Hotel Amsterdam. In the end, it wasn't about the hotel. It was about trying to stay connected, trying to feel close, trying to make sense of something senseless. Even in moments like these, perhaps especially in moments like these, we're just doing our best to carry on with love.

Following our stay in Amsterdam, we travelled to Maastricht not just as part of the holiday or for the music, but to honour Mum and Dad. They had loved André Rieu's concerts, and this trip felt like a way to stay connected to them, to hear the music they loved, to create a moment of remembrance wrapped in something joyful. We used to joke a lot about Mum and Dad liking these concerts because they were often the younger ones in the crowd and André played 'old people's music'. But they loved his music, and now we had the chance to witness his talent for ourselves.

The concert itself was everything people said it would be – beautiful, grand and filled with warmth. Vrijthof Square, where the open-air concerts are held, seemed to glow with life and music. People from all over the world gathered in celebration. But for us, it wasn't just entertainment. It was something more personal, something more significant yet beautiful to celebrate.

During the concert, Australia-Dutch soprano Mirusia Louwerse stepped forward to sing *Wishing You Were Somehow Here Again*, a song already so heavy with longing and grief. As she sang, she looked toward us. It wasn't staged or planned; it just happened, a moment of connection in the middle of a crowd of thousands. For that moment, it felt as though she wasn't singing to the audience, but to us specifically. To our loss. To our heartbreak. To Mum and Dad. Even though Mirusia would have sung that song many times over, it was heartfelt and meaningful to us. In that song, I felt the weight of everything we'd carried from Brisbane to Maastricht. But I also felt something lighter – the reassurance that love doesn't vanish.

It finds its way into music, into memory, into unexpected moments on warm European nights.

That trip was never about seeing a concert. It was about finding a way to say, 'We remember. We miss you. We carry you with us still.'

Maastricht 2015

We stayed at a hotel overlooking Vrijthof Square, right in the heart of Maastricht, where the concerts unfold each year beneath the towering presence of the Basilica. From our window, we could look out over the square, see the stage being prepared and watch the buzz of anticipation grow each day. It felt special to be there, as though we were connected to Mum and Dad not just through the music but through the very place itself. We sat in the crowd for one night, and on the other nights we could watch from the open window of the hotel room. In some ways, it was like a corporate box.

One of the unique things about André Rieu's concerts in Maastricht is how meticulously they are filmed. Every show, every angle, every face in the crowd is captured on camera. Before the concert, we had the opportunity to meet with André's son, Pierre Rieu, who plays a key role in running the productions. Pierre was almost as big a deal as André, and during our conversation, he had media following him and filming. Pierre handed us something we hadn't expected. It was a DVD with footage of Mum and Dad in the crowd from the concerts they had attended.

Someone, somewhere, had taken the time to carefully go through the footage, to find our parents, and to work out exactly where they had been sitting at two shows they had attended. And there they were, Mum and Dad, smiling, laughing, enjoying the music, living a moment of pure happiness. To see that, captured on film, was a gift beyond words. It gave us something tangible to hold onto, proof not just that they had been there, but that they had been happy. And how grateful we were to have had parents who embraced those moments so fully.

The following year, in 2016, we got to meet André when his orchestra came to Brisbane. Mirusia arranged for the meeting following one of the shows, and we got to go backstage and meet quite a few of the team. It was a highlight for our daughter Sophie, who was playing the violin at the time. It would have been a highlight for Mum and Dad as well; they would have loved to have been there.

Amsterdam has become a key part of our story. It is known for its nightlife and red-light district, but beyond the city centre, Amsterdam is a beautiful city with so much to offer. With years of service and anniversaries to come, Amsterdam will be a big part of my future.

Saying goodbye

It seemed like a long time coming, and during those first few weeks, we were not certain if we would ever get the chance to say goodbye. But we did, and it was emotional and draining. I will always be grateful for having the chance to say goodbye properly to my wonderful parents.

By the time we got to the funeral, we were well prepared for the ceremony and the service. We had already been through the memorial service in August, followed by our impromptu service at Westgaarde in early September. What the service in Westgaarde had done was prepare us for the funeral. We had already experienced seeing Mum and Dad in the caskets – a moment of reality that hit me hard. It was still difficult the second time around, but less, which gave us a chance to get the funeral done.

For the funeral, we had the two videos with photos and music we prepared for the memorial service, along with a couple of speeches already done. Paul Reis was our celebrant again, and we just needed to write the eulogies. From the date of the death, we had ten weeks to prepare. As we had done for much of those last ten weeks, we were determined to do everything for Mum and Dad together, so we booked a double time slot and held a joint service.

Mum and Dad's funeral was held at the Albany Creek Crematorium on September 25, 2014. Albany Creek Crematorium was a place that, over the years, had become part of our family's history. It's where they were both cremated, in a simple and dignified ceremony that brought together friends, family and a community still coming to terms with the enormity of their loss. The funeral itself ran well, but there were always reminders of the actual scale of our parents' deaths. When we arrived, there was a huge bunch of flowers that had been delivered, with a little card from the Prime Minister's office. We had ordered sunflowers for both caskets and placed several items and keepsakes alongside the bouquets. I remember looking at those two caskets and thinking about what they had been through to get to this point. A remarkable journey that ended that day in the cremation chamber.

Matthew and his brothers at the funeral at Albany Creek

There was something familiar about the Albany Creek Crematorium. Dad's parents had been cremated there, and in the coming years, so too would Mum's parents. The crematorium was accommodating to our needs; we were able to leave Mum and Dad's ashes in safekeeping until we were ready to scatter them at Mooloolaba the following May. There's a strange peace in knowing that this crematorium has cared for our family over generations, as each chapter has ended. I suppose, in a way, it brings a sense of continuity, even in the face of something so brutally sudden and senseless.

Following the service, we went back to the Eatons Hill Tavern for some drinks and something to eat. The venue of the memorial service, some six weeks earlier, was the perfect place to catch up with family and reflect on the last ten weeks.

What follows is the eulogy David delivered in honour of Mum at the funeral. These words say so much about who she was and how much she was loved. This eulogy was written by David with input from Adam and me.

> I will start by reciting one of Mum's favourite quotes: 'Life is ten per cent what happens to you and ninety per cent how you react to it.'
>
> Susan Marilyn Horder (nee Black), our mum, was born in Brisbane on October 9, 1951, and grew up in Chermside. She lived in Albany Creek for much of her adult life.
>
> A loving daughter to Rex and Joyce Black and sister to Peter and Julie.
>
> Mum grew up at Hilltop Avenue, Chermside and attended Wavell State High School. Mum went to teaching college and taught at Stafford State High School before retiring when her first child was born in 1975. I remember her telling me that she used to get the entire classroom to line up and show her their fingernails to make sure they were trimmed. That has stuck with me. I am not sure you would be

able to get away with that today. Mum's patience, sensibility and her natural caring nature would have served her very well in this role. Growing up, she was always correcting our grammar, manners and etiquette. The school teacher never left her. One look from Mum and we would behave.

A mother to Matthew, David and Adam. Grandmother to Sophie and Joshua. Sister-in-law to Glenn; mother-in-law to Holly and Natalie; and relative or friend for many others.

Today is our chance to say thank you, Mum, for the way you brightened our lives. We all feel cheated that you were taken from us so young, and yet we must learn to be grateful that you came along at all. Only now that you are gone do we truly appreciate what we are now without, and we want you to know that life without you is very, very difficult. We have all despaired at your loss over the past two months, and only the strength of the message you gave us through your years of giving has afforded us the strength to move forward.

Always a Susan and never a Sue, you were an inspiration for others when it came to dealing with grief and death. The 'no face angels' were a symbol of your strength during these hard times. We have one of your angels here with us today, reminding us of our own inner strength to deal with your loss.

Ironically, Mum was not afraid of dealing with death. When her loved ones passed away or were facing life-changing battles, she was a pillar of strength and support. Rather than ignore and hope someone else's pain and struggle would go away, she confronted it head-on and offered continuous and loyal support. Some of you are in this room today. Looking through her sent emails over the last months of her life, I was overwhelmed at the heartfelt messages she had sent to some of you. Constant communication, and even during her recent travel, Mum was thinking about those she loved. Rather than just enjoying her precious overseas adventure, she was thinking about others and, at the same time, appreciating her life. Perhaps that will be Mum's legacy. All the decisions she and Dad made were centred on those they loved. I believe they had the perfect balance of looking after themselves alongside their family and friends.

The last time I saw Mum was in London on June 26, 2014. In typical fashion, she was concerned for my wellbeing. She was reluctant to move on to the next part of her trip, to stay and take care of me. Top of the list was my nutrition. Mum has promised to make a list of the things I should be eating and the foods I should avoid. It was something I took on board, as the day before their fateful flight, I had stocked the fridge in my flat with an array of healthy foods and was ready to embark on a change that was needed. In the end, that food got left behind as I flew out for Australia to be with my brothers.

It's these little reminders that we will miss the most, although we will always have the thoughtful advice of our mother in the back of our minds.

As many of you know, very few people were as organised and thoughtful as Mum. When staying at Mum and Dad's place over the past couple of months, I was blown away at some of the things I came across. She has a birthday diary with a list of everyone's birthdays. She would never forget a special occasion. In this diary, she lists the gifts that she purchased for everyone over the past six years. This way, she would not buy the same gift again. In the linen cupboard, I found a box of gifts. Only mum will ever know who these gifts are for.

I unfortunately did not inherit this talent; I remember ringing Mum one year for a catch-up, completely oblivious that it was her birthday. In return, Mum gave me a birthday book with everyone's birthdays in it.

Mum also kept a personal diary – we found diaries from about the last ten years. In them she wrote down all their daily activities, appointments and social engagements. She also has made a note of every time she spoke with me whilst I lived overseas. On some dates she writes 'David called', on other dates she writes 'David called, and it was a nice chat'. It made me laugh; some chats must have been more challenging.

How incredible for her to record those memories. She did the same for Matthew and Adam. We all went to Mum when we needed information about a date, a memory that needed clarification. Mum would know. So, we will use these diaries to get this information moving forward.

I had many chats with Mum over the phone during the last thirteen years. We would talk about everything. She would listen, never judge and always offered me guidance but was never domineering. I will really miss being able to pick up the phone and hear her voice. Not once, not even once, did Mum complain or not sound interested in hearing my news.

In 1972, Mum married her soulmate, Howard, or Dad as we liked to call him. She was just twenty years old. A union that would last to the end, some forty-two years. It is a small comfort that Mum and Dad were taken together, as there was no Mum without Dad, no Howard without Susan. Mum and Dad had a partnership in every sense. Rarely in disagreement and always consistent in their thinking and decision-making. Mum played a big role in this and stood by and supported her husband in all facets of her life.

My mum always supported my dad and allowed him to follow his ambitions. With every success my father had in his life, my mum was the backbone. An incredibly strong, loyal, caring and sensible woman. Never one to jump the gun – she gave thought before she spoke and always displayed a constant level of common sense. Mum never needed a lot of people around her; she had found her best friend in my dad. Mum also really enjoyed her own company and really enjoyed her space.

We were never in doubt that Mum's priority was her children – 'the boys'. Be assured, looking after us was a full-time job.

We always had a packed lunch for school. When mum fell pregnant with Matthew, she stopped working as a school teacher. Mum had a full-time job of bringing up three very different personalities (personalities that have served us very well over the past couple of months).

Mum was always there – I remember other school friends whose mums used to work. I had no idea at the time how lucky we were. Every school event, her tuckshop duties, school runs, school fates, Mum was there. Not once did we ever have to know or feel what it was like to not be cared for and supported during our school years. Every afternoon we would run down the street from Albany Hills Primary School, and Mum would be there with afternoon tea – pikelets were our favourite.

Mum loved the simple things in life – reading books, walks along the beach and along the waterfront at Sandgate, swimming, barbecues, keeping fit with aqua aerobics, their favourite Thai restaurant, peeling prawns, Facebook and Coffee Club.

She would want us today to pledge ourselves to caring for her beloved parents, Rex and Joyce and her grandchildren, Sophie and Joshua. Mum dedicated much of her recent years to caring for these people close to her heart.

Grandma and Grandpa, we cannot imagine how you feel. You raised a wonderful daughter who you can be proud of. Mum got the best of each of your aspects, not least of which was her love of travel. Exploring new and interesting places was one of Mum's favourite things to do. From international trips to caravanning at Mooloolaba. In recent years, Mum would use her iPad to research the best parts of local attractions and decide on the best course of action.

Mum was known as Gran to Sophie and Joshua. Mum thought the world of her grandkids. She couldn't wait to visit when Sophie was born. When my parents' eldest, my brother, Matthew, phoned about Sophie's birth, Mum (and Dad) wasted no time in taking the drive to

Nambour to see their first grandchild. It was the same when Joshua was born. In fact, they never wasted any moment they could to see the children. Birthdays, special occasions were always important and were never missed.

While reflecting on Mum's extraordinary life, I researched the name Susan. What I found was quite interesting and more than appropriate for our mum.

> *'Susan means graceful lily. Susans are open-minded and honest. Susans make excellent companions. If properly taken care of, a Susan will give you love, friendship and laughter. Susans are extremely loyal. Susans are extremely fun, caring, intelligent, very funny, beautiful and make the best friends ever. Susans are the epitome of classiness.'*

I don't think anyone can argue any of these points. I think these words really sum up Mum's character and relationship with her friends.

Mum was always a private person, so to know her well was an honour and a privilege. Mum would not be overly pleased with all the fuss that has been made over her; however, she would be proud of the response from all.

Matthew, Adam and I are incredibly proud, very proud of our mum. She lived her life with honesty and integrity. We are glad that you could all share her life with us. She will always be fondly remembered and never forgotten.

Perhaps the last words should be left to Mum. In an extract from an email Mum sent on July 16, 2014, the day before their fateful flight, Mum wrote:

> *'As we always say, enjoy yourselves while you are well, make the most of life.'*

Rest in peace Mum xx

Just as we did for Mum, Adam found the words for Dad when none of us knew quite what to say. His eulogy, delivered with strength and grace, captured not only Dad's character but the legacy he left behind. I include it here as a tribute not just to our father, but to the love we all shared. This eulogy was written by Adam with input from David and me.

As I started this eulogy, I wondered how I would ever sum up sixty-three years of Dad's life. I realise no matter what I come up with to say about him, it won't do the scope of his life justice, for he had a full life and was loved by many. I also speak today on behalf of my brothers, Matthew and David.

The immense loss we felt on July 17 will always be there and words can't describe the pain and continued sadness we, and many of you, continue to feel. However, today we honour our father and have a chance to offer thanks for the great years we all got to share with him.

Our father was a wonderful man. He was a father, husband, brother, grandfather and friend to many people. I always admired my father and had a great deal of respect for him. The following words cannot describe how much he meant to us.

Howard Ramon Horder (or his royal highness – HRH) was born on October 30, 1950, at the Royal Women's Hospital in Brisbane to Norman and Ethel Horder. It's fitting that Dad's parents are resting in this same memorial park, and I'm sure are with Mum and Dad today.

A father to Matthew, David and myself; brother to Glenn; grandfather to Sophie and Joshua; son-in-law to Rex and Joyce; father-in-law to Holly and Natalie; and relative or close friend to many others.

Dad spent most of his childhood growing up in Chermside on the same street as Mum, but did have some time in Wodonga, Victoria as well.

He attended Wavell State High School.

It's hard to talk about Dad without mentioning my mum. They loved and lived as one. They showed, by example, how a marriage should be and that finding true love was possible. Most importantly, they were best friends and just so compatible.

After getting married in 1972, they quickly settled down and built their first home in Albany Creek a couple of years later. Not long after that, Matthew was born, followed two years later by David and four years after that, I came along. We were all born in March, very organised.

Our father was a very hardworking man. Whether it was work in the office, house, yard or family, he never stopped. His work ethic was something to be admired. Before his career kicked off, he was working two to three jobs to pay the bills, which allowed Mum to stay at home with Matthew at the time. He was working as an insurance clerk Monday to Friday, and at night and weekends, he would mow lawns and concrete driveways.

Dad's career spanned four decades and he achieved so much in that time. Mostly Dad worked in the life insurance industry, finishing off in financial management planning. Over these years, he pushed himself to achieve more and more and challenge himself in ever-demanding roles. There were periods where Dad was working long and hard hours to provide the life we had. Dad was extremely selfless and lived by one driving ambition, which was to provide for his three boys and his wife. What a great job he did, and an amazing example to leave the three of us. He was funny at times and would be very quick to say 'No, you don't need that' if we wanted something. But of course, most of the time, he would cave in, and none of us went without. He was a big softie at heart, and Mum knew how best to play the game, which was always entertaining. In 1991, when we all moved down to Sydney (as a family), Dad purchased Matthew, David and me our own television for our rooms. This was a big deal but resulted in the three of us staying in our rooms.

I know his industry colleagues and friends held Dad in high regard as a trusted and professional man.

Some of our fondest memories of Dad came from our caravan holidays. He loved caravanning and, in his later years, leading up to retirement and after, the caravan was back and better than ever. In the last couple of years, Dad did some write-ups for a caravanning and motorhome magazine. I will read you Dad's last article and words:

'We have been caravanning since 1982, when our children were little. Nowadays, post-retirement, it's just the two of us, and we spend up to four months each year in a caravan that bears little resemblance to the '80s version. Susan and I particularly enjoy coastal regions where we can share our love of swimming and relaxing happy hours, looking out over the ocean, glass of wine in hand, and thanking our lucky stars that we are able to enjoy this wonderful lifestyle in Australia's climate. We laugh a lot, and often just the two of us! Laughter is the best medicine, coupled up with regular exercise. We try to walk a good distance and pace every day, which helps compensate for the happy hours.'

I can't think of anyone who would care for possessions more than Dad. Anything he owned was kept in immaculate condition, and if by chance it wasn't, he would have a tool or gadget to repair it. When that wasn't enough, it would be in the bin and moments later replaced with a new one. His caravans have always been the perfect set-up with everything you could possibly need, and all kept perfectly. Once set up on site, Dad couldn't rest until absolute perfection was achieved, but I think this tinkering and playing around with stuff entertained him and was part of the attraction. At times, this provided the people observing with much entertainment.

He was a dedicated father and more than any words spoken here can demonstrate. Throughout the years, as parents, their roles evolved, and we were always fully aware of the love they had for us. Dad loved Christmas and loved helping Santa on Christmas Eve. Year after year, he would set the scene ready for Christmas morning by putting grass in the bucket of water left out for reindeer and some half-eaten carrots and one year, I remember sleigh marks on the lawn. Not sure how he managed that, but it is a special memory. It was his attention to detail that helped make Christmas a special family memory.

He also involved himself in our sporting endeavours and as a child I played cricket. Dad didn't know much about cricket, but that didn't stop him contributing his time and knowledge. I remember one year in under twelves, he was the assistant coach and umpired. Since cricket wasn't his strong suit, I wasn't surprised when he gave me out LBW when clearly the ball itched outside the leg stump. I wasn't impressed, but there he was supporting me on the weekend after working hard all week. It's only when you get older you understand the effort involved and truly appreciate the support like this. There was never a sleep-in – Dad was always up and doing something – he did not stop. His home was his castle.

As we grew older, his efforts focused heavily on making the effort to ensure his three children were happy in life and had everything they needed. The highlights of their later life were the opportunity to spend time with friends and family. As you are aware, travelling was one of their favourite pastimes, especially if it involved seeing one of their children. They took several trips to London to see David and me, and it was no coincidence that their favourite caravanning spot was close to Matt, Holly and the kids.

I have always shared the passion for cars that Dad had and thoroughly enjoyed some of his more exciting vehicle purchases. The highlight was the '98 Subaru WRX STI Type R coupe, which he bought in New Zealand. At the time it was very rare and very quick and turned many heads. I remember my school friends wanting to come over for joyrides around the suburbs of Wellington, which had some great winding roads. This flame-throwing turbo brought me much enjoyment, and I know Dad loved it. This was just one of many cars Dad owned, and all were treated as his pride and joy. I will miss talking cars with Dad, and one day I had hoped to get my own WRX equivalent and would have loved to take him out.

Dad also loved his golf and was a member at Wantima Country Golf Club and played in the Saturday comp with his good mates, John, Garry and Nigel. If you attended the celebration of life, you would have heard some great stories from those boys, and I know Dad thoroughly enjoyed their company.

Dad was a proud grandfather. Over the last eight years, the addition of Sophie and Josh to our family brought Mum and Dad much happiness and fulfilment. Dad loved being a pa and was incredible at the job. Matthew and Holly will dearly miss this irreplaceable role.

I don't think there was a person who met him who didn't like him. I've heard from many people that he was such a genuinely nice guy with a good heart who easily accepted you in his life. He was generous with his time and helped those who needed it. He also had a sense of humour and loved to tell a 'good' joke. I thought about sharing one today, but the only ones I could find were too dirty to repeat here. If any of you were on Dad's email list, you know what I'm talking about.

His words of wisdom were: 'Be thankful for what you have and enjoy each day you're given. And don't get upset over the little things because it's simply not worth it.'

His legacy is this – the love he gave his family. And I want everyone to know and to remember that this was his greatest gift. I am grateful that Dad showed us what to value in life: that if you put love and family in the centre of it all, you will have a life that is full and well-lived.

I think one of the hardest parts about the sudden loss of my parents was seeing Mum's parents in the aftermath. Seeing their daughter and son-in-law's lives destroyed broke Grandma and Grandpa. They were in their late eighties. They still lived in the same house they moved into on their wedding night, the same house where they raised Mum and looked after their grandkids, including me. To know that their eldest daughter would never walk back into that house must have been heartbreaking.

For Grandma, it was more heartbreaking, given her dementia diagnosis. It was a long road ahead for Grandma, and not the way you should live out your final years. Grandpa was stoic, apart from that day his daughter was killed. He would show little emotion and was full of common sense. Following Mum and Dad's death, I would spend a lot of time with Grandpa chatting about all things, his life, the footy and the lessons he learned along the way. He became a great role model of how to treat people and how to live your life. The way he cared for Grandma was the true definition of 'til death do us part'.

You are not supposed to say goodbye to your kids like that; it's not how it works. Grandma and Grandpa could not travel much in those days; they couldn't get to the memorial service in Melbourne, nor the repatriation. So, to be able to go to the memorial service at Eatons Hill and the funeral at Albany Creek was so important for both.

When it came to the scattering of Mum and Dad's ashes, the choice was simple. One of their favourite pastimes before their deaths had been travelling in their caravan. The last caravan trip they took was during April 2014 at the Mooloolaba Beach Caravan Park, just a couple of months before they flew out to Europe. The beachfront park was one of their favourite places to stay and it wasn't unusual for them to stay four times a year or more. They loved visiting Mooloolaba because they could back the van up to the ocean and get absolute waterfront views. Plus, the added advantage of coming to the Coast was that it was close to my home, which meant they could see us and spend time with their grandkids. Sophie and Josh made so many wonderful memories at that caravan park, which is no longer there. It was bulldozed to make way for a public park and boardwalk. I know this change would have upset Dad a fair bit because they had so many special moments there, but it is now a lovely park for all to enjoy.

On this trip in April 2014, I was walking on the beach out the front of the park with the kids and Mum and Dad. It was a beautiful afternoon; the sand gave way to rocks, and the kids were having a wonderful time peering into the rockpools. As we were walking, Mum casually said, 'If anything should happen to us, we would like our ashes put here at the rocks at Mooloolaba.' I fobbed it off at the time, telling her not to be silly. I honestly didn't believe anything was ever going to happen. For whatever reason, Mum felt compelled to tell me at that time.

It was during that first week after our parents' deaths that I decided to share that story with my brothers. I took them to the same beach, near those rocks. We had a short walk before settling in. It was a nice winter's day; it's a beautiful spot at that time of year. We were sitting quietly, and a huge lump formed in my throat as I tried to control the emotion of it all. I had trouble speaking, and I wasn't sure how I was going to share this very important wish of Mum's. I had Mum's voice in my head.

Out of nowhere, Adam said, 'Wouldn't it be nice to put Mum and Dad's ashes here, near the rocks at Mooloolaba?'

'Did Mum say something to you?' I replied, as the hairs stood up on the back of my neck and my spine began to tingle.

'No.'

'That's what Mum told me last time we were here. I bought you guys here to tell you.'

It was surreal, like Mum was talking to us. I had never experienced that sort of feeling before. In many ways, Mum, on this occasion, prepared us for what was needed.

A few days later, we found more information in the dossier prepared by Dad, which conformed to Mum's wish: 'Should anything happen to us, we would like our ashes placed at Mooloolaba near the caravan park.' So, in those early days we knew what to do; all we needed were the bodies back from Ukraine. Our path was laid out for us, and while it took some time, it was a little bit of clarity in a very clouded mind. And what helped most of all was that the three of us were all united in our thinking – Mum had done her job well with us.

On May 9, 2015, some ten months after they passed away, we placed the ashes at Mooloolaba. It was a small ceremony, just the three of us in a boat we borrowed from a generous friend. It was a beautiful service and respectful. When I think back, we hosted a large memorial service with around 700 in attendance, followed by the joint funeral with one hundred and twenty in attendance, so to say our final farewell with just the five of us, with a few people watching from the shore, was a special way to say goodbye. Mooloolaba will always have that significance and hold a special place in our hearts. I'm lucky that I get to visit Mooloolaba on most days, and I think about that moment on the rocks with Mum every time I am there.

Mum and Dad don't have a dedicated memorial as such. No headstone, no plot in a cemetery or crematorium; their ashes have been placed at sea. Mooloolaba is a beautiful place to sit and remember them. Mum and Dad's names have been included with all two hundred and ninety-eight victims in the National Monument MH17 in Amsterdam and included on a memorial plaque with the Australian victims in the Eastern

Gardens of Parliament House in Canberra. The plaque at Parliament House was officially unveiled by the Prime Minister on the first anniversary of the downing. The Australian Government hosted the families for a service in the great hall, with many similarities to the National Day of Mourning, before moving outside to pay our respects in the Eastern Gardens. It was a lovely service and a great tribute to the Australian victims; however, my strongest memory from that moment was how bitterly cold the Canberra winter was.

Dad had played golf most of his life, and as he got older and into retirement, he competed with his mates in the weekly competition at Wantima Country Club. Understandably, his golfing mates and members of the club were affected by Mum and Dad's passing. The members and the club organised a memorial plaque on the tee of the ninth hole,

Memorial plaque at Wantima Golf Club

together with a memorial garden. A permanent reminder for them at a place Dad loved.

It's a quiet place, and it's not public, but a little something for just the two of them. In addition to the ninth hole, Dad's playing buddies also worked with the club to name one of the regular annual competitions after him: The Howard Horder Stableford Event. Played over four rounds throughout the year, the event is a terrific tribute to Dad, who was always handy in Stableford events. The competition even has its own honour board on the club room wall in memory of Dad and, of course, to recognise the winners.

I had played golf with Dad at Wantima and, every now and then, got the chance to have a round in the Stableford in his honour. It is a special place, and I know that Dad is watching, especially when I tee up on the ninth tee.

The golf course isn't the only place where Mum and Dad are honoured and remembered. On July 17, 2017, three years to the day after MH17 was shot down, the National Monument MH17 was officially unveiled in Vijfhuizen, the Netherlands. The site, just north of Schiphol Airport, is not just a place of stone and metal but a living, breathing memorial. In a field shaped like a ribbon, symbolising both remembrance and connection, two hundred and ninety-eight trees were planted, one for each life lost, including Mum and Dad. The trees form a green ribbon shape, surrounding a central steel memorial engraved with the names of the victims. At its heart is a striking design – an eye, always open, reflecting both the grief of those left behind and a watchful, enduring memory that refuses to look away.

The monument was unveiled at a ceremony attended by the Dutch King and Queen, Prime Minister Mark Rutte and more than two thousand family members, friends and officials. It was a moment of solemn dignity and shared sorrow. Across the Netherlands, the service was broadcast live on national television, and while official viewer numbers were never released, it was estimated to have been viewed by more than four million people; watched by those who had lost loved ones, those who felt connected to the tragedy and those who simply refused to forget.

What struck me most about the monument was its scale, set in approximately two hectares of parkland. The trees will grow long beyond our lifetimes, although Mum's tree had to be replaced two years later as the park settled. Beneath them, the ground holds not just roots, but memory. A place where strangers come and stand silently and leave knowing that the victims of MH17 are not forgotten. The monument isn't just for those we lost; it's for those of us who go on, carrying them in heart and story. A place for us to remember and reflect on what we have endured. As I said, the park is not far from Schiphol Airport and the runway where the fateful flight departed. When you sit in the memorial, you can see and hear the countless planes that come and go through one of Europe's busiest airports.

The Dutch have always been respectful of the dead when they host and hold ceremonies, and one of the most respectful things they do is read out the names of every passenger and crew member who has passed away. At significant milestones and events, surviving family members can read out the names of their loved ones. So, on this occasion, we were offered the chance to read Mum and Dad's names out and of course I accepted. When accepting, there was an option on the form asking whether I was prepared to read out any other names on behalf of family members who would not be in attendance. I ticked yes, thinking that it would be for other Australian family members who were unable to make the trip to the Netherlands for the opening of the National Monument MH17.

Two days before the event, just as we were arriving in Amsterdam, I received my list of names. There were seven on the list for me to read –

Mum and Dad's, and five other victims from the Netherlands. And, as you can imagine, they were very Dutch names. For anyone who knows me, I have enough trouble speaking English, let alone a foreign language, or pronouncing words with a different dialect or accent, so I became quite anxious quickly. I also knew how important it was to read the names of those lost for the loved ones who couldn't be there, so I needed to do it justice.

*Reading the names of some of those lost at
the opening of the MH17 memorial, 2017*

During our earlier travels to Amsterdam, we met an artist named Sara and her husband, Kevin, at the Rembrandt Art Markets in Rembrandtplein (Rembrandt Square). Kevin worked as a translator and had happened to work for KLM – the official Dutch airline – on the day MH17 was shot down. KLM was a code share on that flight, so Kevin had been busy that afternoon supporting family members trying to find out information on the flight during those first few hours. I thought that if I could speak to Kevin, he could help me phonetically spell out the names, which would help me read them out.

I knew that those markets weren't on, but I also knew that Kevin and Sara also frequented the Museum Market. So, I jumped on a push bike and rode down to the market, and through pure luck, there was Kevin and his daughter, selling Sara's artwork, at one of the first stalls I visited.

Kevin was great. I showed him the list of names and instantly, I had the support I needed from a familiar face who I could trust. I probably could have asked anyone in Amsterdam for help that day, but it was nice to be able to call on someone who already had a connection with us and knew the sensitivities around reading the names. We wrote them out on a bit of paper, so I had it ready for the next day.

I am glad I did. As with many MH17 services in the Netherlands, it was broadcast live on television and streamed worldwide. And, in front of members of the royal family and Mr Rutte, I was able to confidently pronounce those names with the dignity and respect they deserved.

Going to court

Dad's dossier got us started with the early advice we needed, and we were fortunate to have Susi O'Reilly on our team, managing the estate and other affairs for my brothers and me. There was a lot of comfort knowing that Mum and Dad had everything in order. Some matters could only progress so far until we had a death certificate, and getting that certificate had taken a while, as we didn't have the bodies.

In the end, we received two death certificates each for Mum and Dad. One Queensland death certificate and one from Ukraine. Understandably, the Ukrainian death certificate was written entirely in Ukrainian, so it was accompanied by two sets of official translations. As it was translated in the Netherlands, the first translation was into Dutch, followed by a second translation into English. The translations were officially sealed with stickers and stamps. I'm not sure if we will ever need the Ukraine death certificate, but we have them nonetheless, and it is ultimate proof that Mum and Dad were killed in Ukraine. The Queensland death certificates arrived in October 2014. The Ukrainian versions arrived a couple of months later, in December.

Apart from the languages, there were noticeable differences in each. The Queensland certificates listed the place of death as Flight MH17, Donetsk, Ukraine and stated the cause of death as an 'injury sustained in high altitude aircraft disruption' – the description provided by the Victorian coroner. While the Ukrainian death certificates were more specific on the place of death, listing Ukraine, Shakhtarsk district, Grabove village. These certificates did not state the cause of death.

But we were dealing with something much bigger than finalising the estate; we were embroiled in something international. Our parents had been murdered in such a horrific way, and someone was responsible for that. Suddenly, terms like the Montreal Convention and international aviation law were being thrown at us – matters we'd never heard of before, yet now they potentially carried enormous weight in our lives. What did these things mean for us? They weren't abstract legal concepts; they determined what investigations could take place, who was responsible for them, and even how our parents' remains would be returned home. They dictated the process, the timelines and, in some ways, how much control we had. We needed an aviation lawyer to represent us appropriately and, more importantly, to represent Mum and Dad's interests. Ultimately, our interests. Given that I needed legal advice on so many things, I really needed someone in my corner.

Within a week or two of my parents' passing, I was approached by legal representatives purporting to be from the airline, trying to influence us. There were also many aviation lawyers vying for our business. Some of the latter were what I would call 'celebrity lawyers', who were vocal and in the public eye, citing previous cases and various legal jurisdictions. Often, they would try to influence our thinking with big payouts and promises of justice, but beneath the surface, there was not much to look at, just motherhood statements and previous cases that didn't seem relevant. In the end, I talked to a lot of them. I was after someone who was experienced and measured. After much consideration and in consultation with my brothers, I decided to go with John Dawson from Carneys Lawyers (he has now moved to Vector Legal). John and his associates were a good fit for our family. Their experience in aviation and connections overseas were significant, and their ability to navigate the complexities around the international legal matters was just what we needed. It was comforting to be able to call on someone to provide advice and guidance on all the matters coming our way. This decision supported our needs and took a load off our shoulders throughout this period.

Not only did we have representation in Australia, but we also had support overseas. Internationally, we were fortunate to be represented by a legal team appointed by the Dutch Government to look after all families. Our representative was Antoinette, a compassionate and highly capable lawyer from Legal Tree in Amsterdam. She was engaged to represent our family in matters relating to the crash and the broader legal processes that unfolded in the Netherlands, including the criminal trial and proceedings before the European Court of Human Rights. Antoinette's guidance, professionalism and humanity helped us navigate an incredibly difficult matter. She has become more than just legal support; she has been a wealth of knowledge, a steady presence and a friend in the Netherlands during a time of uncertainty.

During this period, I remember feeling a little less anxious. I had been able to engage representation to support our needs. So much of what happened was out of our control and for a fleeting moment, I felt like we had a say in the way forward and help with the long road ahead.

One of the most significant undertakings in those early days was the air safety investigation led by the Dutch Safety Board. These investigations are typically done after all air accidents, following a set protocol, and are intended to improve air safety. This investigation was a crucial first step in establishing the facts of how and why the plane was brought down.

While in those early days it seemed clear what had happened, there was also significant misinformation and various theories being spread. Given the complex geopolitical backdrop and the inaccessible crash site in eastern Ukraine, the investigation was conducted under extraordinary circumstances. Despite the challenges, the Dutch Safety Board approached the task with precision and conducted three investigations into the downing of flight MH17.

The final report, released in October 2015, confirmed what many had feared: flight MH17 was struck by a Russian-made Buk surface-to-air missile, launched from a rebel-controlled area in eastern Ukraine. The missile detonated near the cockpit, instantly killing the flight crew and causing the aircraft to break apart mid-air before falling to the ground in thousands of pieces, killing all passengers on board. The report also raised serious questions about why civilian air traffic was still permitted over a known conflict zone and recommended stronger international protocols for risk assessment and airspace management. The 'MH17 Final Report' was the first confirmation that a missile had brought down the plane; it had always been the leading cause reported in the media, but this was the first time a formal report with the findings was published. The report, for the first time, described what passengers on the flight may have experienced. As a relative, it is almost incomprehensible to fully understand what my parents went through without feeling sick in the stomach. The MH17 crash brochure that accompanied the report, summarised the findings as follows (Dutch Safety Board, 2015):[2]

> The impact was entirely unexpected, which means that people were barely able to comprehend the situation in which they found themselves. There was hardly any time for a conscious response. The occupants were exposed to extreme factors almost immediately. Depending on variables such as the occupants' location in the cabin now of impact, the factors were not the same for all the occupants.

Several occupants immediately sustained severe injuries because of the factors, probably causing death. For others, the exposure caused reduced awareness or unconsciousness within moments. It could not be ascertained at which exact moment occupants died, but it is certain that the impact on the ground was not survivable.

While the final report was not intended to apportion blame, its work laid the foundation for future legal proceedings. It provided critical evidence to the Joint Investigation Team, a multinational criminal investigation involving the Netherlands, Australia, Belgium, Malaysia and Ukraine. The Dutch Safety Board's findings gave the families of the victims, including ours, an official record of the truth and a degree of certainty about what had occurred.

More than just a technical document, the Dutch Safety Board report was the first formal acknowledgment of the scale of the injustice. For many of us, it validated what we already believed but needed the world to hear – this was not an accident, it was an act of violence with consequences that demanded accountability. To truly seek justice, we wanted to know who was responsible and to hold them to account.

While the Dutch Safety Board focused on how MH17 was brought down, a parallel and much more emotionally charged process unfolded through the JIT. This team worked across borders and legal systems to piece together one of the most complex aviation crimes in modern history using the findings of the investigation and evidence gathered by their team.

The JIT determined early on that MH17 had been destroyed by a Buk missile system transported from Russia and launched from an area controlled by Russian-backed separatists. Their investigation was methodical, drawing on a wide range of sources including satellite imagery, intercepted communications, witness statements, forensic analysis of the wreckage and even social media posts. The evidence had to be verified to ensure it was authentic, as the investigation was flooded with false claims.

More than one-and-a-half million pieces of evidence needed to be checked. It was slow, at times painfully so, but for families like ours, it was vital; an assurance that justice was not being forgotten or delayed without cause. Also, it was impossible for the families of the victims to complete; we needed the support from the JIT, including Australian officers, for this to happen.

In 2019, using the extensive findings from the JIT, Dutch prosecutors charged four individuals – three Russian nationals including a former colonel of the Russian Federal Security Service and two former Russian military intelligence officers and one Ukrainian – for their alleged roles in the attack. They were accused of orchestrating the transport and deployment of the Buk missile launcher. I have chosen not to include their names in this book because it doesn't sit well with me. One of the former Russian military intelligence officers was the only accused to have legal representation and participate in the trial, while the others were tried in absentia.

The trial itself, held in a secure courtroom near Schiphol Airport, became a long, sobering journey. It was hard living so far away from the court; we followed the trial from the other side of the world. The differing time zones were a factor, as the hearings were livestreamed, mostly at night, and not conducive to good sleep. I can't remember how many times I wished I were closer so I could participate in the proceedings firsthand. For years, we waited for the day when the world would officially hear what had been done to our loved ones, not just as victims of circumstance, but as people caught in the crosshairs of geopolitical cruelty. The courtroom became a place where truth was spoken aloud, on the record, and preserved in history.

Under the Dutch legal system, family members of the victims were afforded the right to speak, something I had never experienced before. It supported our written Victim Impact Statement and provided an opportunity to speak directly and publicly to the court. This had an emotional impact on me but was also deeply healing.

This was somewhat made more difficult than first thought, as the original plan to travel to court in Amsterdam and speak in person was initially curtailed due to Covid-19, with many countries around the world, including Australia, shutting down international travel in a bid to contain and eliminate the virus that seemed to be spreading like wildfire. We had all our flights and accommodation booked, ready to go. Court dates were adjourned, and proceedings were delayed, taking longer than anticipated, as was the case for many things during Covid. Ultimately, our flights and accommodation were cancelled and we were unable to travel to be in the courtroom in person. However, finally, after many months, on September 7, 2021, at ten o'clock in the morning, I had the opportunity to speak via livestream from home to the court in Amsterdam. Here is what I said:

Right to speak – Matthew Richard Horder, following the murder of his parents, Howard Ramon Horder and Susan Marilyn Horder.

Good morning,

I wish to share part of my story that left my mother and father murdered, and what followed is now a seven-year investigation involving pretrial hearings and many months of waiting. I hope to explain how it has affected me. It is hard to describe in a few paragraphs every moment of despair, every anger-filled day, all the lost time, the unanswered questions, the permanent psychological scars. There is much frustration in writing this statement, while those responsible, including the Russian Government, walk and act freely as if nothing happened, while continually spreading misinformation about their involvement and preventing justice from being achieved in a shorter timeframe.

To attempt to describe the full impact of this crime is unreasonable, but here goes. It colours all aspects of my life, though none of it can be measured. If only there were a way to gauge the pain caused and a way to assess the damage. How do you measure all the conversations I have missed out on with Mum and Dad? How many visits week in, week out? How many trips to see my children, my parents' grandchildren?

My parents were hard-working Australians who never asked for anything. They were active, healthy and enjoyed life. They cared for their elderly parents and their young grandchildren. They loved to travel both domestically and internationally and, ultimately, this cost them their lives.

Without a doubt, one of the most difficult things I have ever had to do was tell my kids that their grandparents' plane had been destroyed and that they had both been killed. How can you imagine the despair on my children's faces when they think about their grandparents and how they were so callously murdered without justice, justice that is seemingly improbable? Unfortunately, I don't need to imagine as I see and feel it through my children daily.

The stress it has put on my family and personal relationships is enormous. It has taken a huge toll on the trust I have in others. The perception I have of the world has been changed. My pessimism has increased, my ability to experience joy has decreased. And all my suffering transfers to those close to me, which transfers to those close to them, and so on. These impacts are immeasurable on career aspirations and quality of life. On any given day, it takes enormous effort to function and maintain what I have got.

On June 8, 2014, my immediate family and I spent the day with my parents, enjoying a picnic and walk just outside of Maleny in the Sunshine Coast Hinterland. Little did I know that that would be the last time I saw them alive.

Two loving parents and grandparents would set off on a trip overseas to enjoy their retirement, something they had done many times. It is a part of retirement that everyone is entitled to enjoy.

On the morning of July 18, 2014 (Australian time), I woke to panicked messages from my family. I spoke to one of my brothers, who had told me our parents' plane had crashed. In an instant, my whole life changed, and my heart was broken. His message was confirmed by constant images on television – 'No survivors', it said. Very quickly, it became evident that this was no accident, rather an act of murder on a grand scale. An unspeakable tragedy that civilians travelling on a commercial aircraft should never have to endure – yet my parents are dead, and I endure it day in, day out.

My parents were active in our lives and with my children. They loved being grandparents. They were much more than my parents; they were carers for their ageing parents, providing ongoing love and support for those around them. They provided advice on everything from gardening to financial services; you name it, they were part of our lives. These facts are important in understanding the impact of their loss and how I feel every time I think of them and every time this tragedy is mentioned.

When I first heard about my parents' death, I felt incredible loss, a headache that lasted for weeks, a headache that returns whenever the flight is mentioned. A headache that sits with me to this very day.

I will never forgive Russia and those responsible for the actions they have taken against my parents and the actions they have taken since. The crime they have committed and the lies they continue to spread, some seven years later, and counting.

Mentally, every day is a struggle. The sudden loss of anyone close to you will always have a lasting impact on your life. The mental struggle is exacerbated by the length of time to be able to identify our parents' bodies and to get them repatriated and home for a funeral. And the length of time taken to seek justice and answers. I have been diagnosed with post-traumatic stress disorder (PTSD), depression and anxiety directly because of this incident, thus confirming my daily battle.

In speaking with you today, I would like to share with you some words from both my mother and father. It is important to me that I read out what they have said as they cannot be here for themselves. Their voice can still be heard here in court, even in their death.

In 2010, on Dad's sixtieth birthday, we had a special day with the immediate family to celebrate together. Dad gave a great speech as only Dad could, and I would like to share a small part with you.

In speaking about this milestone birthday and his future in retirement, Dad said:

'What's in store for the future? Hopefully enjoying good health and enjoying participating in the growth and development of our grandchildren, Sophie and Josh, and travelling both in the caravan and overseas where possible.'

He went on to share some tips from his life experiences. These included:

- Take calculated risks – you never get ahead without taking some risks.
- Being too conservative is negative.
- Don't become a workaholic.
- Get balance between work and family.
- And always take holidays.

My parents were terrific grandparents to my kids, and they loved to travel. They lived up to Dad's words and enjoyed life at every opportunity.

This next piece is a letter that my Mum wrote to Dad back on January 17, 1969, before they were married and when they had just started seeing each other. I have the original copy of it right here in Mum's beautiful handwriting. Dad had kept it all these years, and now we still have it some sixty-two years later.

In it, she says, 'We'll have to get together again. I don't know about you, but I enjoyed it the other night. It was fun just talking, laughing, I should say, even though Dad went out looking for us and nearly had the police on our tail.'

Their love for each other was evident at this time.

Three years after writing that letter, Mum married her soulmate when she was just twenty years old. A union that would last to the end, some forty-two years. It was small comfort that Mum and Dad were taken together, as there was no Mum without Dad, no Howard without Susan. Mum and Dad had a partnership in every sense. Rarely in disagreement and always consistent in their thinking and decision-making. They stood by each other in all facets of life.

I am forever grateful for the thirty-nine years I got with my parents but grieve for the lives that were denied at the hands of the Russian Government. My heart breaks knowing that my parents never got to fully live their retirement. For their age, they were fit and healthy and full of life. This crime has shattered and devastated our family.

I miss my parents every day; however, there is nothing that can be done to bring them back. It is vitally important that those responsible are held to account and that the criminal proceedings are fully completed through to the end. I will never understand why this has happened to me and my family, and while I do not have high expectations, I sincerely hope that it never happens again.

In the lead-up to the verdict in 2022, we were offered the opportunity to visit the reconstructed wreckage of MH17. Nothing could have fully prepared me for the experience of standing before the shell of an aircraft pieced together from thousands of fragments, resting within a cavernous hangar at the Gilze-Rijen Air Base in the Netherlands.

The Dutch Safety Board had led this painstaking reconstruction effort, using recovered wreckage from the crash site in eastern Ukraine. The reconstruction was an important part of the report and, of course, supported the JIT in providing some of the evidence needed for the criminal trial. They transported the twisted metal, torn fuselage and shattered windows back to the Netherlands and, over time, began reassembling it like a jigsaw puzzle, perhaps with a few pieces missing. The result was a partial reconstruction of the forward section of the plane, cockpit, business class and part of the economy section, mounted on a steel frame, hauntingly incomplete yet disturbingly vivid. Mum and Dad had been sitting in row two in business class. The steel frame allowed you to walk inside the reconstruction, and we found ourselves standing in the destroyed aircraft, exactly where Mum and Dad's final moments were. It was a moment in my life that I will never forget.

This wasn't just a mechanical task. It was a tribute to the lives lost and a tool for truth. Every bolt, wire and panel was examined for signs of what had happened on that fateful day. And in that effort, one of the most crucial breakthroughs came from a detective sergeant within the Australian Federal Police.

During a meticulous search for the wreckage in Eastern Ukraine, the AFP officer identified a small piece of metal that matched the holes in the fuselage in the cockpit section of the plane, a fragment from a Buk missile warhead. This tiny, distinctively shaped shrapnel shard matched the kind used in the Russian-made Buk surface-to-air system. Ultimately, the metal fragments were forensically tested and matched back to the factory where the missile was fabricated. It was a breakthrough moment, helping investigators move from theory to undeniable evidence.

Reconstructed wreckage, standing where Mum and Dad were sitting

Standing in front of the reconstructed aircraft, I found myself looking at every little detail. All the holes and cracks in the plane. The multiple edges told the story of the missile's detonation, how it exploded near the cockpit, killing the crew instantly and tearing through the plane. The noise and chaos at that moment the warhead detonated must have been horrific. As a family member, it was devastating. I was already heartbroken, but looking at the aircraft just broke my heart even further. As someone seeking justice, it was also profound. The reconstruction was as remarkable a feat as it was horrific. This reconstruction had become the silent witness to a crime, giving voice to the two hundred and ninety-eight people who could no longer speak.

For me, the wreckage wasn't just a technical artefact. It was the place where my parents had spent their final moments. It was where lives changed forever. And yet, through the incredible dedication of so many, from Dutch engineers to Australian investigators, this wreckage had become the very thing that helped the world see the horrific truth, clearly and unequivocally.

More than eight years after MH17 was shot down, on November 17, 2022, the District Court of The Hague delivered its long-awaited verdict for the criminal trial. It was a day of relief and profound emotion, and I was at the court in the Netherlands to witness the verdict. The court found three of the four accused guilty of murder and sentenced them to life imprisonment. The fourth individual accused, one of the former Russian military intelligence officers, was acquitted on the grounds of insufficient evidence tying him directly to the missile launch.

The verdict mattered, not because it reversed what had happened, but because it publicly recognised that this was an intentional act and that people bore responsibility. For the families, it was a moment of validation. The world saw what we knew in our hearts, that our parents, our loved ones, had been stolen from us in a brutal and unlawful act, and the perpetrators were not faceless; they had names, roles and now, legal consequences.

Still, it was bittersweet. At the time of publishing this book, the convicted men remain fugitives, unlikely to ever serve their sentences. Russia refused to extradite them or take any responsibility for their involvement. But for many of us, this verdict wasn't just about punishment; it was about accountability, truth and recognition. We had walked a long road to get to this point, and while it didn't bring closure, it brought something perhaps more valuable: a global, official acknowledgment of the injustice we'd lived with for so long.

For the first time, we had a guilty verdict through a court of law. It was factual and proven; no one could take that away from us. In some way, I felt I had done my part to support the case. I exercised my right to speak, an emotionally draining moment in time, but to get an answer to many of our questions was a quiet satisfaction.

I walked out of the courtroom and saw my lawyer, Antoinette. We smiled and hugged. Victory was sweet, and this had been eight years of hard work for her. It was a happy moment amid horrific circumstances.

I, along with four other Australians, was interviewed for Australian TV, broadcast live back to Australia, which was waking up to the news of the successful verdict. There was no time to prepare, just straight into it. The interview was quick, and I reinforced why it was important for our family to have the truth proven in a court of law and why it was important for me to be a voice for my parents. Once again, this was a headline story and seemed to be the only news of the day.

Interview for Dutch TV at the
MH17 Memorial in Amsterdam

Nearly eleven years after the loss of MH17, a formal acknowledgment came from the highest international aviation body. In May 2025, the International Civil Aviation Organization (ICAO) Council handed down a historic decision, finding that the Russian Federation had breached international aviation law in relation to the downing of the flight. For me, and I imagine for many others who lost loved ones, it was a moment of further validation and deep emotion, especially as so much time has passed.

The ICAO Council ruled that Russia had violated the Chicago Convention, the international agreement that prohibits the use of weapons against civilian aircraft in flight. It seems somewhat ridiculous in the first place that we even need an international agreement that prohibits the use of weapons against civil aircraft, but here we are. It was a wrongful act, not just a tragic consequence of war. It was murder at the hands of Russia.

The ICAO Council decision, reached through joint efforts by the Australian and Dutch governments, including DFAT lawyers, confirmed that our case was 'well founded in fact and in law'. After so many years of pain, legal battles and sometimes feeling like we were shouting into the void, we were heard. This ruling doesn't undo what happened. But it matters. It means Russia can now be formally held accountable, and the path to seeking reparations, while unlikely, is no longer merely symbolic.

It doesn't bring closure exactly, but it does offer a recognition that's long been missing. As someone who lived with the grief and shock every day, it felt like the world finally caught up and saw our loss not as an unfortunate headline, but as a breach of fundamental principles. Principles that were meant to protect people like Mum and Dad, and families like ours, from exactly this kind of heartbreak.

I am not someone who journals, in fact, I never have, but on reading about the ICAO Council judgement, I had a moment of reflection and wrote a few things down.

'How did I feel? I knew it was coming; we had plenty of emails and updates from DFAT, but it still plays on you some eleven years later. I can quite easily say it had little impact on me, but that would not be telling the full story. I was grumpy and irritable all day. I woke up earlier than normal and felt like every little thing was not going my way. You could say I handled it okay, but you never really know how these things are going to play out. I felt out of alignment; my neck hurts and I had that lingering headache again. It is probably best described as a PTSD reaction.'

However, rather than accepting the ICAO Council's ruling, Russia took the case to the International Court of Justice (ICJ), the principal judicial organ of the United Nations, to challenge the decision. The ICJ appeal does not overturn the ICAO Council decision, but it suspends the decision's legal effect while under review. In short, Moscow continues to deny any involvement in the MH17 tragedy. The decision to appeal is hurtful. The weight of all the findings to date provides more than enough evidence to confirm what happened, and the appeal provides zero credible alternative evidence to suggest anything different.

Russia had continued to reject any blame, challenging the official investigations that linked its military to supplying separatists with the surface-to-air missile system. But the truth came out.

On June 17, 2025, we received notice that the European Court of Human Rights would hand down its findings on July 9, 2025. Given the criminal trial and the ICAO judgement, there could be only one outcome. The evidence hadn't changed. But we still waited anxiously.

The European Court of Human Rights was unanimous in its judgment. Russia had violated the right to life by its involvement in the shooting down of flight MH17 not only by failing to cooperate, but by actively opposing the investigation into the disaster. In the eyes of the European Court of Human Rights, Russia has also treated the relatives inhumanely, the court stated. The European Court of Human Rights summarises this inflicted suffering as follows[3]:

> 'The next of kin of the crash victims had suffered profound grief and distress on account of the killing of their loved ones and the aftermath of the crash. Because of Russia's refusal to arrange for the crash site to be secured, it took eight months to complete the recovery of the bodies. Some next of kin had had to bury the incomplete bodies of their relatives; in some cases, body parts had been returned to them after the burial had taken place. In two cases, the victims' bodies had never been recovered. The Russian authorities' continued denial of involvement and their failure to carry out an effective investigation had prolonged the agonising wait for answers for the next of kin and had aggravated their suffering. The character and dimension of their continuing suffering had been sufficiently severe to amount to inhuman treatment.'

Being treated inhumanely, in our case, has nothing to do with being physically hurt. It's about being ignored, dismissed or treated as if your loss doesn't matter. That's how it's felt dealing with the Russian Government since the downing of MH17.

For more than a decade, I have lived with the grief of losing my parents in what was an avoidable tragedy. But what's made it worse is the way we've been treated since. There's been no ownership, no real acknowledgment of what happened and no compassion from those responsible. Instead, there have been lies, delays and a refusal to tell the truth. When a powerful state like Russia refuses to cooperate, enforcement is limited and that reality is painful.

It's hard to describe what that does to a person. It's like being made to feel invisible, like your pain is inconvenient. There were times when it felt like we weren't even allowed to grieve properly because the politics and denial took over everything. Some of the commentary that circulated when the findings and judgments were handed down was quite hurtful. Things like, 'We always knew it was Russia', 'That's old news', 'Tell us something we don't know' and 'Nothing will ever come of it'. But it makes a difference to the victims' families. Multiple independent bodies (JIT, Dutch courts, ICAO and the European Court of Human Rights) have reached the same conclusions, proving once and for all what we may have known. That truth cannot be altered any further.

I have never wanted revenge, although at times I felt like it. I've just wanted the truth to be recognised and our parents' deaths to be treated with the dignity they deserve. What I've faced instead is silence, excuses and a complete lack of respect. That's what being treated inhumanely feels like; being left to carry the weight of something that should never have happened, while those responsible turn their backs.

The landscape of loss

After years of investigation, legal proceedings and international scrutiny, there was finally a verdict, in fact, three decisions through the highest levels of accountability possible. There was justice, on paper, but it didn't bring Mum and Dad back. It didn't fill the empty chairs at birthdays or Christmas; it didn't stop the silence that follows the mention of MH17 in a conversation. The world saw who was responsible. But there was no real sense of triumph. There were no real celebrations. Perhaps some relief but still emptiness. A sense that after all the fighting, something had finally been acknowledged, but at a price we never wanted to pay.

This wasn't a victory we asked for. It was one we were forced to pursue. And in the end, even justice felt hollow, because we never got to share it with the two people we love the most. The pursuit of justice continues, as I am sure it will for probably the rest of my life.

It probably goes without saying but my life changed forever. How do you live with grief? How do you deal with sudden loss? When will this ever end? Will I get over it? There is no simple answer to any of these questions, and responses change over time. For example, if you asked me these questions ten years ago, I would have responded very differently from how I do today. My response will also evolve over the next ten or twenty years. This is because the response is shaped not only by what you've experienced, but also by the knowledge and wisdom you have collected after it. I have no doubt that I will learn more, even just from writing this book.

I have heard from people in the past that I have been good at dealing with tragedy, but it's not a fair assessment; I don't think you *can* be good at it. It is easy to see, in retrospect, how the different moments in my life, in some ways, prepared me for this, along with how I was raised by my parents. I didn't realise it at the time, but looking back, I was perhaps equipped to handle situations I never dreamed would happen to me. Mum was very good at handling death; she always seemed to know how to respond and what to say when someone she knew passed away. Perhaps some of that has rubbed off on me.

In my lived experience, you never really know how grief is going to impact you or when the next wave will slam into you. I am certain that it is enduring. As time goes by, those waves seem to be further apart. But every now and then, it comes through quicker, almost like a tsunami, as if to remind you that grief is still there. You learn to let grief sit alongside joy, love and hope. It doesn't replace those things, but it changes them. It sharpens your awareness of what matters. It softens you in some ways, hardens you in others. Over time, you come to understand that tragedy doesn't shrink. What grows is your capacity to live around it. You must learn to live around it; otherwise, it will drive you to despair.

When I look at our situation, my two brothers and I have had different experiences and handled things differently. I still have trouble understanding how we managed in the hours, days and weeks that followed the tragedy. I especially think of David and Adam, and how they have managed the situation we faced; they are incredible human beings.

While the actual circumstance was the same for all three of us, nothing else was – the grief was different, the connection to our parents was different and our personal lives were all different.

You learn to understand that grief is not the same for everybody. And when you extend that understanding out across the rest of our family, our extended families, the other victims and families, you get thousands of different grief reactions from the one event.

Now I am pretty sure what I am describing is not earth-shattering news, and no doubt there are countless research papers confirming my observation, but I felt compelled to share this aspect of my story to show you what I do with grief and how it shapes who I am today.

Firstly, I have learnt – and am still learning – how to cope with milestones. For the past eleven years, on the anniversary of Mum and Dad's deaths, I have had a different experience every time. For the first couple of years, that frustrated me; I thought I could anticipate what would happen and be ready for it. But you can't. What you *can* do is let go of expectations and the need for you to feel or act a certain way. The strength is in knowing that you will come out the other side and will be fine. It's a new normal, but you will be fine.

Secondly, when you have that lived experience, it influences how you treat others. I am a better leader, a better manager and, for the most part, a better father and partner. When you understand that people's reactions are all different, you can manage and accept that difference in all its forms. The result is that you become more compassionate and understanding.

Living through tragedy changes you not just in the obvious ways, but in how you move through the world. It shifts something in your thinking. You become more aware of what others might be carrying, even when they're smiling, even when they say they're fine.

I'm more aware that people's reactions to stress or difficulty don't always make sense on the surface. Someone might be short with you one day or shut down the next, and it's not always about the job at hand. It might be something at home, a silent struggle or grief that hasn't found its voice. That sort of understanding doesn't come from reading a book; it comes from living it.

In my own case, I carried a lot of weight after losing Mum and Dad. And in that process, I realised just how unpredictable grief can be, not only for myself but for everyone around me. Some days I was composed; other days, angry, hollow or overwhelmed. I didn't always behave how I would've wanted to, and I could never predict how I was going to behave. Some days, I still can't. A great example is Father's Day. It is a day that I could almost do without because it reminds me of what I don't have. But at the same time, I've had to show up for my kids as a father. I know that I have been irritable and cranky on Father's Day, and it shows. I am sure the kids wonder what they have done wrong to upset me. Of course, they have done nothing wrong; it just seems to be a day when I can't control my feelings. I can't seem to compartmentalise the moment, being a father as opposed to having a father. This realisation helps me see the power of people showing patience, of not needing an explanation before offering support. I try to lead with that same kind of patience now, and maybe one day the kids will see that.

The reality is, I don't get everything right, but I now see the value in just being present, in listening, in making space for others. I understand more deeply that resilience isn't about being tough all the time. It's about acknowledging what's hard and still choosing to keep going, to keep caring and to keep showing up for the people around you.

People often tell me I'm resilient. They also say I'm calm, particularly in a crisis or a difficult situation. But I know the resilience is real. It is a feeling as much as an action. It's something that's been built piece by piece throughout my life. Looking back, I can see how much those early experiences shaped me. For example, when a flight gets cancelled, and you miss an important engagement, there is no point flying off the handle; it is better to deal with the situation and work out what is possible. After all, a cancelled flight is better than a dead flight.

Undergoing open-heart surgery as a seven-year-old was an interesting one. At that age, you don't fully grasp the risks, but you learn early on how fragile life can be. Later, when in Los Angeles during the earthquake, I again saw how quickly the ground beneath you, literally and figuratively, can shift. Those experiences, in their own way, were hard at the time, but they planted those vital first seeds of resilience.

Losing Mum and Dad was a completely different level of pain and loss, but I think those earlier challenges in life gave me some foundation. I just didn't know it then. Those incidents taught me that I could survive hard things, even when they felt impossible. Resilience isn't about never struggling; it's about finding a way to keep going despite it all.

People also talk about my calmness, and while I don't always feel calm inside, I do know how to stay visibly steady when it matters. Leading a patrol in surf lifesaving has been a great example of that. You learn quickly that when you're responding to a rescue or helping someone in trouble, panic doesn't help anyone. You must project calm so others can feel safe. But you also draw on what you know, what you learnt in training and the annual proficiencies. It all kicks in and that helps keep your calm. In a strange way, my early life experiences kicked in and helped keep me calm when I needed it. Chatting to the Prime Minister felt easy; it just happened. That same mindset has carried into the rest of my life, whether leading teams at work, being a parent or facing personal adversity.

There is no doubt that my upbringing was one of the largest influences on my life. I saw through my parents how to be resilient. They didn't teach me, they *showed* me. Mum was always calm. Dad was less so, but he had an incredible ability to adapt and change.

These experiences haven't made me bulletproof. They've just helped me understand that resilience can be shaped, and that you can grow into it. It's not something you're born with; it's something that life teaches you. If I've managed to lead through loss or stay composed under pressure, it's only because I've had to. I've learned that you can still be vulnerable and be strong at the same time. I don't always feel strong and sometimes I come unstuck, but I keep going. And that, I've learned, is what a resilient heart is.

If resilience is about standing strong when the storm hits, tenacity is what gets you through the long, slow grind that follows. It's that stubborn part of you that refuses to quit. Looking back over my life, I can see that tenacity has carried me through some of the hardest chapters. I think it took me years to see it and start to understand it, but it's there.

Again, recovering from open-heart surgery as a child required more than physical healing; it required the slow, patient determination to bounce back when it would have been easier to sit out. It meant turning a difficult start into something purposeful. That recovery taught me not to expect quick fixes, and that improvement often comes step by step, not in giant leaps. As a child, you don't think about tenacity. It's just innately there. Seven years of growing up with appointments and tests was a slow grind, but I made it to fifty and I'm still going.

Years later, in the wake of MH17, I didn't have the luxury of shutting down. Grief doesn't operate on a schedule. Life just kept moving. I had to keep showing up for my family, for my kids, for the practical demands of organising a memorial, managing the repatriation process and dealing with governments, the media and legal systems. There were days when it felt overwhelming, but I kept going, not because it was easy, but because I didn't want Mum and Dad's story to end in silence. And deep down, I knew I had to keep showing up so others would too.

After the downing, I returned to work. For some, it may have been earlier than expected, but there were no rules. It wasn't because I had fully healed – you know now that grief doesn't work like that – but because

I knew I had something to offer. And work is part of reality for most of us. Being part of something purposeful helped me keep moving. My workplace gave me structure, and in return, I brought my whole self, changed, yes, but also more grounded, more aware. Work was never the same as it was before, and it never will be.

I lead and work differently now. I listen harder. I notice more. I understand that sometimes, just turning up is the win. I've seen how kindness in the workplace matters, especially when someone is just trying to hold it together. In those early months, I didn't always have the right words, but I had purpose. And purpose is a powerful guide.

As a leader, I often tell colleagues to 'keep moving'. It's simple, but it says everything. When the red tape gets heavy, when the task feels too big, or the pressure mounts, that's my reminder, to myself and to the team. You don't have to solve everything today. You don't have to be perfect. Just take the next step. Keep moving. That's where momentum builds. That's how change happens and how you help others. That's how we lead through uncertainty.

Tenacity doesn't always look heroic. Sometimes it's just showing up to a meeting, making a phone call or writing the next page. It's answering the email, having the hard conversation and staying in the room when things get tough. Maybe it is showing up on Father's Day even when you don't want to. It's not about being fearless, it's about carrying on, even with the fear and the weight of what you've lived through.

Tenacity is also about staying the course when no one's watching. Whether it's following through on a long-term commitment, helping steer complex programs or volunteering in lifesaving and community organisations, I've learned the value of steady, persistent effort. Leadership isn't always dramatic. Sometimes it's just turning up again and again, especially when others can't. It's about committing to something larger than yourself and holding your ground when it counts. For me, it has meant continuing to honour my parents' legacy, raising my family with heart and purpose and leading with integrity even in times of uncertainty.

I wouldn't say I've always felt strong. But I've kept going. And in the end, that might be the truest measure of tenacity – moving forward, even when it hurts, even when it's slow and even when no one else knows how hard it is.

Grief and mental health are deeply connected. When you lose someone, you don't only experience emotional pain; it affects your thinking, your energy and your motivation. Pretty much everything. It can cause depression, anxiety, trouble sleeping and even physical symptoms. You feel like you're going crazy, but you're not. Your brain is trying to make sense of a world that doesn't make sense anymore. One day you feel okay, the next you can't get out of bed. It can isolate you, overwhelm you and leave you stuck. That's why acknowledging it, seeking help and acting matters, because untreated grief can turn into long-term illness. Sometimes you feel like you need to fight it alone, especially when those around you are going through the same grief. Here's the thing, though: you don't have to fight it. Having people with the same understanding, in my case, my brothers, can be beneficial. In a way, they get it.

Early on, when I started to realise I wasn't okay, I made an appointment with my doctor and received a referral to a psychologist to address my mental state. It wasn't just grief that I was experiencing; it was something deeper and more persistent. The psychologist talked through a whole range of things with me; there was a lot of talking. And for some of it, I couldn't understand why there was a need for discussion. I explained the event and what I was going through. At one point, I remember the psychologist showing me a prism; the prism was my life and everything was in order. Then, one day, someone turned my prism on its side, and all parts of my life were no longer in order. I just looked at the psychologist.

'My life is not a triangle, mate, it's a lot more complex than that. Can you start doing your job, please?'

Probably not my finest moment, and it highlighted why I was there in the first place, but I don't think the answer was in a textbook. Eventually, I went through a series of questions and answers that informed a more direct assessment. The result was that I was showing signs of anxiety, depression and PTSD. I must admit, it was hard to hear, but I needed to hear it as it set me on the right course to manage it.

For a while, I didn't really know what any of that meant in practical terms. I just knew I wasn't getting the sleep I would normally get. I was constantly on edge. My thoughts felt foggy one moment and overwhelming the next. Little things would trigger big emotional responses, and sometimes I couldn't explain why. I had never experienced this previously. There was this weight, mentally, emotionally and physically, that I carried every day. And while I was trying to hold it together for everyone else, inside I was starting to struggle.

The PTSD caught me off guard. I hadn't been on the battlefield or in the wreckage, but I had lived through the trauma of MH17 in a very real way, one that was also very public. I think sometimes it is hard to explain a PTSD reaction. I wrote these things down one day to help explain how it feels for me. In April 2025, I said goodbye to my daughter, who flew out to Melbourne to live. It was an exciting opportunity for Sophie and I didn't know where it would take her. In the end she moved home, but in that moment when I watched her flight take off, I felt that sense of helplessness.

'I think it's normal to be a bit sad when a child leaves home. And for the most part, I have been very good at sharing Sophie's excitement about her next move. Sophie flew to Melbourne from the Sunshine Coast. The moment that really got me was when the plane took off, and I immediately had that sense of dread and sadness. At the end of the day, that is how my parents were killed, and to see her flight take off really set me off emotionally. I tend to keep this to myself and keep it in, and to be honest, it doesn't always last long, but it's there, and I can't change it. To say it doesn't affect you is a little pointless. For the rest of the day and indeed for the days to follow, I was on edge, less productive and just generally exhausted.

'When her flight took off, I could feel the air leave my lungs, my heart racing. It wasn't just worry, it was a full body response, a surge of panic and a dread that felt impossible to reason with. In that moment, my brain didn't care that it was a different plane, a different day, a different world. The fear gripped all the same. I couldn't stop checking the flight status, refreshing the screen until the plane landed. That's what PTSD does; it doesn't ask permission, but just arrives, uninvited, dragging the past into the present. I don't tell anyone, and I especially don't tell Sophie. I keep it to myself; I convince myself that it is the best way. Sophie doesn't need to carry my fear; she has her own. I put on a calm face and talk about the weather. It feels safer somehow to stay silent. But the silence is loud inside me.'

I used to wonder how some people in their lives really lost control. Alcohol, drugs and behaviour not generally accepted by society. But I can see how it could happen, how things can spiral out of control quickly. Not deliberately, but out of desperation. Trying to make things better or soften the pain in some way. I could see myself at various times being dependent on that stimulus or the next hit. I was looking for that afternoon drink. It would take the edge off. One would become two and then three. I would catch myself doing it and stop, although sometimes I would convince myself it was okay, like I deserved it. *Life has dealt me these cards, so I can do whatever I want.*

In the past, I never looked for that afternoon drink; it wasn't needed. It's the same with food, perhaps worse. It doesn't help that I have a sweet-and-savoury tooth. If it's there, I can get the hit of dopamine I need. Self-control becomes the biggest issue.

We all get stressed at some time, and some level of stress is a normal part of life. At different times, I can feel my stress levels going up. However, for the most part, I feel my stress levels are within normal limits. But looking back, I can see various scenarios where the events around MH17 would trigger me. For example, every time I saw a plane, I would experience heightened stress. If I saw a Malaysia Airlines plane, it would be next level; it would take me back to that moment when I spoke to Adam, to the connection to Mum and Dad and to what happened to them. It was horrible but bound to happen at different times. You are never ready for it and believe me, it catches you out every time.

For a period there, I would have copious anxious moments connected to Mum or Dad. I might hear a voice in the crowd that sounded like one of them and turn around only to find they weren't there. Or I would see a face in the crowd and think that it was Mum or Dad. I was always so disappointed when I realised it wasn't them, but for a moment it felt real. In many ways, I think their presence was there, whether it was in the energy around or just in me.

One night in Amsterdam, in the lead-up to the trial verdict, I was in bed trying to sleep, but I couldn't. I could feel my breath and feel my heartbeat. I was having a panic attack. I could feel my chest tightening. I felt restricted, restless and on edge. And the more I couldn't sleep, the worse it got. To make matters worse, I knew I needed some sleep to prepare for the huge day ahead. The fact that I wasn't sleeping just made it worse. I didn't know what to do, so I called a friend back in Australia, not family, but someone who knew me well enough and had the right words for me. After five or ten minutes, my friend reassured me to settle a bit and said it was okay to feel that way, especially given the stress of the previous seven years. It's a lot to ask of a friend, so I'm lucky that I had someone to call and it helped.

I think I was so tired that I eventually fell asleep. The next morning, I woke up exhausted. But I got out of bed and went for a walk. It was a simple action, but one of the best things for me. I've learnt over time that moving my body helps. It gets the endorphins flowing and that works for me. Sometimes, if I know I'm going to be triggered, I will get it in early, almost as if I am prescribing it for myself.

Anxiety can sneak up on me in the most ordinary of moments. It's not always loud or dramatic. Often, it starts with a simple feeling of being trapped. I might have a fear of being confined or claustrophobic. It might be tight clothes pressing against my chest, a knot between my shoulder blades pulling on my spine or standing in a room that suddenly feels too small. Sometimes it's a crowded train, a packed venue or just walking into a space where I can't easily see a way out. I become hyperaware of everything. How my shirt feels, how close the walls are, how little space there is to move. My chest tightens. My back tenses. The air feels heavier, like there's not enough of it to go around. My breath shortens. It's not a full panic attack; it's more like my body is on high alert, sounding alarms and I can't shut off.

It's worse when I find myself in a situation where I can't easily leave, like on a plane, a long train ride or stuck in a car. When there's no quick exit, the feeling can intensify. Just knowing I have no real way to escape can send my anxiety spiralling. It's not the destination that worries me; it's the inability to move or get space when I need it. For me, anxiety is often about space, or the lack of it. It's the fear of being cornered, unable to breathe or settle.

Over time, I've found ways to manage it, such as wearing looser clothes, sitting in the aisle seat or near exits when possible or using breathing techniques. But some days, I still just must ride it out. Remind myself it will pass. That I can breathe and I will find space again.

I remember feeling sad often early on. It goes without saying that you will feel sadness when you lose someone; it's a normal response. I also remember telling myself that it is okay to be sad, but it wasn't okay to stay in the sadness. I don't know where I got that from, but in essence, if I were feeling down, I would recognise it and do something to address it.

It could be as simple as getting out of bed and having some breakfast, as opposed to just staying in bed all day. The act of getting up to eat breakfast meant my day had started. *I might as well do something else.* Don't get me wrong, I allow myself to be sad and feel the sorrow, but I don't want to live my life in sadness; it's horrible.

Some days, it's more than sadness. For me, depression is far heavier. It's a fog that rolls in and stays longer than you'd like. Some days, it dulls everything: the light, the sound, even the things I used to enjoy. Other days, it steals my motivation or my ability to focus, like trying to function through mental quicksand. It usually arrives when you least expect it. It can come with tiredness that sleep doesn't fix. With a tight chest, frustration and sometimes a sense of failure, even when I know, rationally, that I've done nothing wrong. It makes me pull away from people I love, even when I don't want to. Some people close to you pick up on it, but mostly it's invisible to others.

I still go to work. I still smile. I still 'function'. But inside, there's a weight. Not always crushing, but present. It can be hard to talk about it, as depression is still surrounded by stigma. I don't think I really understood depression growing up and I hadn't experienced it myself until now.

And yet, through all of this, I've come to learn that depression isn't a weakness. It's part of what happens when life breaks your heart. It's part of what happens when trauma takes up residence and doesn't fully leave. I don't think you can simply get over it; it is something you need to work through. I've had to learn how to live with it, how to manage it and how to speak its name without shame. Some mornings I would lie in bed, knowing I had a full day ahead of me, but feeling as though I was already out of energy before my feet even touched the floor. I'd go through the motions – shower, dress, smile at people – but inside I felt flat, like I was watching life happen through a pane of glass. To counter this, I often plan to exercise in the morning. Maybe a session at the surf club, CrossFit or maybe at the athletics track. The approach changes your mindset straight away. The exercise part is important, as well as the social networks. Often, the weight inside is still there; the routine and mindset help me manage it positively.

In addition to seeking professional help at various points over the years, my main ways of coping with mental health challenges have been eating, exercise and, though less consistently, talking about it.

Eating has become something of a crutch. It's fair to say that I enjoy food and I like to eat out. It's a feature of travelling and often an experience as much as it is fuel for my body. But when I go through difficult periods, eating becomes a way of coping with what I am facing at the time. And for me, it means I eat too much, both in portion size and in less healthy options. I don't always realise it in the moment, but I certainly feel the effects later, usually around my waistline.

It is comfort eating, and I find myself overeating during some of the more difficult times. I should stress, for me, it's not about chasing some ideal body or being thin. It's about being fit and healthy. When I eat in ways that don't support my health, emotionally or physically, it catches up with me in more ways than one. It has been cyclical. I can do well for a period and then slip back. I catch myself justifying the excess, as if to say *I deserve to eat whatever I want.* It is one way of coping, but not always a good one.

Exercise, on the other hand, has always been part of my life. I grew up loving sports, the outdoors and just being active. So, when life got hard, it felt natural to turn to movement as a form of therapy. A walk, a swim, a training session – they're more than just physical activities; they clear my head, give me space to think and remind me I'm still capable of moving forward. Training gives me another purpose; it might be for a charity walk or something more competitive.

For a while, I'd regularly walk up Mount Coolum, a volcanic dome on the Sunshine Coast that attracts keen walkers with its challenging track and promised ocean views. I used to joke that I was off to see my therapist, only this one didn't cost me anything. That walk became a symbol of progress. Step by step, breath by breath, I'd climb my way through whatever was weighing me down. And even if it didn't fix everything, it helped. I can feel the benefits every time, so the challenge is to know when I need it and take the forty minutes to go for the walk. It's a great treatment plan.

I've learnt that talking things through helps, often more than you expect. Whether it's letting go of something that's been sitting heavy or just saying it out loud so it's not swirling endlessly in your head, there's real value in conversation. That doesn't always mean seeing a professional. For me, some of the most helpful moments have come from chatting with a mate, a trusted colleague, or someone in my circle who just gets it. Telling your story to a group of strangers is uniquely healing and captivating for the listeners.

Having a solid social network is gold. People you can be real with, who'll listen without trying to fix you or change the subject. You feed off each other in a good way – honest talk, shared stories, mutual support. It doesn't always have to be serious; looking at the lighter side of life and different situations is important. You need to be able to laugh at stuff, otherwise it will break you.

I'm not knocking professional help; it's important, and I've used it when I needed to. But not every problem needs a therapist. Sometimes, you just need someone who cares and will sit with you in it. That can be more powerful than any prescription.

Triumph in the face of adversity

How can anything good come out of such an atrocity? It does; you just have to choose to find the good. From early on, we could see the value in doing things for others; it feels good, and it is good for the community in which you live, while providing opportunities you may have never had the chance to experience. It started early when we sold pins at the memorial service and donated the proceeds to the Queensland Cancer Council. We could have easily given everyone a pin for free, but raising funds for an important cause felt good. At a time when we had few answers, it helped to uplift us knowing we were doing something positive. It always does.

For as long as I can remember, I've believed in giving back. It's just something that's always felt right. It's a way of being part of something bigger than myself. Sometimes it's been connected to family or a cause that touched me personally. Other times, it's simply been about lending a hand where it was needed.

When I worked at Caboolture Council, which is now Moreton Bay Regional Council, part of my role involved supporting the Sunshine Coast Sports Federation. At first, it was just another part of the job, another committee, another set of meetings. But over time, it became much more. Even after I moved on from the council, I kept showing up, volunteering on the committee and at events, and helping where I could. It became a constant in my life for more than fifteen years.

They surprised me with a life membership in 2015. I remember hearing my name announced and feeling this wave of emotion hit me, more emotion than I would normally have had. It wasn't something I'd ever sought, but it meant a lot. It was an honour, and it reminded me that the small things you do over time matter.

After Mum and Dad passed away, I found myself searching for new ways to give back – something that would help me heal and maybe push me in new directions. That's how I stumbled into a kind of giving that would change my life: adventure fundraising.

As mentioned earlier, I was introduced to Paul Reis, who assisted with the memorial service and funeral. Paul was one of those people whose energy could move mountains or at least inspire you to climb one. One of his specialties was organising adventure fundraising treks. These are multi-day challenges in iconic locations, where participants pay their own way so that every dollar raised goes straight to the cause.

In early 2015, Paul mentioned that he was planning a trek for the following year, walking sections of the Great Wall of China. I'd never had any burning desire to go to China, but something about it stuck with me. Maybe it was the challenge, maybe the purpose behind it. Either way, I told him to keep me on the list.

A year later, I was packing for Beijing.

Our fundraising goal was to support stillbirth research at Mater Little Miracles, a project close to our family, though not something we ever spoke about much. My grandmother, Mum's mum, had lost a baby after Mum was born. I don't know all the details, but from what I've learned, the birth was handled with a lack of compassion that was perhaps more common in those days. The baby was stillborn and taken away. There were no photos, no footprints, no chance for her to say goodbye. She never saw the child again.

As a father myself, I can only imagine that pain. For my grandmother, it was a loss she never recovered from. Mum used to say she'd cry out in the night for her baby. Knowing that, supporting research into stillbirths suddenly felt deeply personal.

The trek itself was extraordinary. Six sections of the wall over six days, each stretch offering something different: ancient stone steps winding through the hills; wild, crumbling sections reclaimed by forest; and long ridgelines where the wall disappeared into the mist. We also spent a day volunteering at an orphanage in Beijing, part of the foundation's commitment to giving back locally.

I raised funds through donations and a few events back home – a high tea at French & Mor, one of Mum and Dad's favourite weekend cafés, a movie night and a music festival called Metal for Miracles.

That last one still makes me smile.

The idea started during a surf with my mate Matt Stewart.

Great Wall of China raising funds for stillbirth research at Mater Little Miracles

'Hey,' he said, 'I've got an idea to help you raise a few bucks for that China trek.'

'What's that?' I asked.

'Let's put on a gig, a few bands, someone's backyard, gold coin donation at the gate. Easy.'

I laughed. 'Alright then, what bands have we got?'

'My band will play,' he said.

'I didn't know you were in a band.'

'Yeah, my brother and I play Metallica covers.'

He left out a couple of small details, like the fact that they didn't have a bass player or a lead singer, but by then, the wheels were already in motion.

Before we knew it, Metal for Miracles had grown from a backyard jam into a full-scale show at The Shed near the Aussie World theme park. We had three bands, The Honourable Members, Blackened (Matt's band) and Holistic, led by Steven Polwarth, who blended new wave and melodic metal. Everyone played for free. The venue donated the space. We had merch, T-shirts, hats, stubby holders and mugs, all to raise funds.

The afternoon was electric. Loud, raw, joyful. Everyone there knew they were part of something that mattered. We raised thousands, but more than that, we raised spirits. People still

Metal for Miracles poster

talk about that night. Matt and I still toss around the idea of doing it again. One day, I think we will.

On the trek, each morning began with the presentation of a yellow jersey, a bit like the Tour de France, awarded to one of the trekkers for different reasons: fundraising, teamwork, spirit. On our final day, Paul called my name.

I was stunned. I hadn't expected it. He spoke about my efforts, not just the amount raised, but the sheer number of individual donors, more than one hundred and forty, which

On top of the Great Wall of China after receiving the yellow jersey

was the most they'd ever seen on any of the foundation's adventure trips. In presenting the jersey, Paul gave quite an emotional speech that talked to the unspeakable tragedy I had been though. I was very proud that morning.

I still have that yellow jersey. I didn't do it for recognition, but that moment reminded me why I give back. Because when you put good energy into the world, it comes back in ways you don't expect.

The following year, in 2017, Paul called again. 'We're heading to California. Six days trekking through Yosemite National Park. Interested?'

How could I say no? Yosemite had been on my bucket list for years, and this time, the cause was dementia research.

It struck a chord immediately. My grandmother, the same one who had lost a child to stillbirth, had been living with dementia for years. I'd watched her fade slowly, her memories slipping away piece by piece. I felt like one of the lucky ones; she always remembered me. But it was heartbreaking to watch someone so strong and kind lose her sense of self.

Raising funds for dementia research felt right. It was something I could do, a small way of honouring her and helping others.

I travelled to California with Ian Toplis, a friend I'd met on the China trek. We arrived a week early, flying into Los Angeles, spending a couple of days in Las Vegas, then looping back to San Francisco to meet the group.

One night in Vegas, my phone rang. It was my uncle. Grandma had passed away.

Even though I'd known it was coming, it still hit hard. She'd been suffering for years, and part of me felt relief that she was finally at peace, but it also brought a rush of sadness and guilt, too. My first instinct was to fly home, to be there for the funeral, to represent Mum.

But after talking it through with my family, I realised that I didn't need to do that. I'd been there for Grandma in life, visiting her every week, helping care for her and Grandpa. That's what mattered most. So I stayed. I recorded a video message from San Francisco and sent it to my uncle to play at the funeral.

Then we began the trek.

Yosemite was breathtaking. The waterfalls were in full flow, the best they'd been in thirty years, the locals said. Snowmelt thundered down the cliffs in the heat of summer. We hiked the Panorama Trail, Mist Trail, Yosemite Falls, Vernal Falls, Nevada Falls, each day tougher than the last. Reaching the top of Yosemite Point, exhausted and drenched in sweat, I looked out over the valley, El Capitan standing like a granite sentinel across the way, and felt a deep sense of peace.

I'd come to raise funds for dementia research, but I'd also come to honour Grandma, and in that moment, I felt like I'd done both.

Yosemite Point raising funds for dementia research

We didn't see any black bears on that trip, despite the signs warning of them everywhere. I remember joking with Paul that they were probably off somewhere waiting for the next group.

Eight years later, in 2025, the year I turned fifty, I went back to Yosemite with my family. The park was as beautiful as I remembered. We retraced some of the same trails, explored new ones and went white-water rafting. On our final day, as we travelled through a meadow in the valley, a black bear appeared, ambling through the grass.

It felt almost poetic, as if the park were giving me a little nod, a reminder that the journey had come full circle.

One of the more memorable charity walks I've taken part in was in support of Hummingbird House, Queensland's only children's hospice, located in Chermside and an auspice of Wesley Mission Queensland.

The walk spanned six days and covered sections of the Bibbulmun Track. The track itself is a stunning long-distance trail that winds through the ancient forests and rugged coastlines, stretching about one thousand kilometres from Kalamunda in the Perth Hills to Albany on the south coast of Western Australia. It's a place full of quiet, earthy beauty, with towering karri trees, misty mornings and long stretches where all you can hear are your own footsteps and the breeze through the bush. Travelling south from Perth, we stayed in the small town of Walpole, which was the perfect place to base ourselves for the trip. Nice walks each day and good food and fireplace each night, a beer or two and a glass of wine. A place to reflect and reset.

Giving back has taken many forms in my life, but the walk along the Bibbulmun Track stays with me the most. It was more than a fundraiser. It was a reminder of how we sit with grief, how we show up when there are no answers, no fixes.

That walk did more than raise money. It helped me grow. It reminded me of Mum's grace in loss, of Dad's steadiness in crisis and of the resilience I had been forced to discover in myself. Grief doesn't vanish; it shifts. It

Bibbilmum Track raising funds for Hummingbird House

finds new places to live inside you, but it doesn't have to take everything with it.

If there is any meaning to be found in tragedy, perhaps it is this: we are changed by what we endure, but we are not defined by it. I have learnt that giving back is not just about helping others. Rather, it has been part of my own survival, a way to honour those I've lost and to keep moving forward. Out of the darkest day came lessons in love, resilience and community. That is what I hold onto. That is what remains.

These experiences have taken me to unexpected places, from a council office in Caboolture to the Great Wall of China, from a surf chat to a heavy metal fundraiser, from heartbreak to healing in the mountains of Yosemite.

Each experience has taught me something about connection, to others, to purpose and to myself. Sometimes the best way to heal is to look outward, to do something that matters to someone else. Because when you give, you don't just change the world around you. You change, too.

Leading in life

I am often told that I have great leadership qualities, but how do you define a good leader? Easy, it might be me. The Oxford English Dictionary describes a leader as 'a person who leads or commands a group, organisation or country'. It suggests that someone is 'in charge'.

But what makes a good leader? For me, being a leader is less about being in charge, rather it is about truly leading. A great leader will delegate to the person or people who are most suitable and put them in charge of a task. And as a leader, I always maintain that I don't know everything; being a leader doesn't make you an expert.

I came to understand the difference between being in charge and truly leading. A title or role can make someone the person in charge, but real leadership reveals itself in how you show up for others in moments of chaos, grief and uncertainty. True leaders are those who provide clarity when there are no answers, strength when others feel lost and calm when emotions run high. They don't just direct, they stand beside you, listen and act with integrity and compassion.

I saw that kind of leadership in the Australian officials who worked tirelessly, not for credit or profile, but to ensure dignity, justice and care for the families. It reminded me that leadership is not about power or position, but about presence. In our darkest hours, we don't remember who held the most authority; we remember who helped carry the weight.

I learned more about leadership than I had in my entire professional career. I wasn't trying to lead; I was just trying to hold everything together for my family and for those around me who were just as broken. It's about how you carry yourself when the world falls apart. It's about showing up, even when you're exhausted and hurting. I saw genuine leadership in the strength of those who supported us, from the officials who worked through impossible logistics to ensure our loved ones were treated with dignity, to the people who asked nothing in return but simply stood beside us. They didn't have to speak loudly or hold a high position to lead; they led through compassion, consistency and care. And in my own way, I did the same. I wasn't looking to be strong. I just knew I had to keep going, for my family, for Mum and Dad, and for everyone who was depending on me to find the next step forward.

When Mum and Dad died, something shifted. In a weird and almost unspoken way, I felt like I inherited the role of family leader. Maybe it's because I'm the oldest, or maybe it was just instinct, but from that moment on, people looked to me. Not for answers, necessarily, but for reassurance, for guidance, for permission to grieve. I became the contact point for so many different people, from our solicitor to the AFP and DFAT. It was a role that just seemed to evolve. I didn't ask for that responsibility, and I certainly didn't feel ready for it, but I took it on because someone had to. In the absence of Mum and Dad, I became the steady voice on the end of the phone, the one coordinating flights, arranging memorials, comforting others while falling apart myself. It wasn't heroic; it was just what needed to be done. And in doing it, I came to understand that leadership isn't about control or confidence. It's about care, presence and love, especially when you're carrying a load no one can see.

So, what makes a good leader, and how can you be a leader when dealing with such great loss? I am a firm believer that good leadership comes from two areas: things you learn and things you are born with. Good leaders don't need to know everything, but they do need to know where to go to get the right information. It might be your team members, or it might be professional support. Once a leader or a manager thinks they know it all, they are most likely going to fail.

So, here are some of my learnings around leadership. It's not earth-shattering.

Care deeply and support others

I've found that when you genuinely care about people, it shows. Whether they're teammates, colleagues or club members, when people know you've got their back, it changes everything. It builds trust. And people tend to give more of themselves when they feel supported. It doesn't take much to care for others, and when you put it into practice, it is almost easy.

Lead by example

You can't expect people to show up, work hard or do the right thing if you're not doing it yourself. People watch what you do more than they listen to what you say. I've always tried to live the standard I expect from others, not perfectly, but consistently. I've also repeatedly used a famous quote that basically says, the standard you walk past is the standard you accept. So, for me to show leadership, you need to be the example.

Take initiative

I've never been one to sit back and wait. If something needs to be done, I'll roll up my sleeves. Sometimes that's meant taking on more than I should, but it's also meant progress. Action breeds action.

Stay accountable

Things won't always go to plan. I've learnt that more than once. But when you own your mistakes, admit what you don't know, and front up even when it's hard, people respect that. Accountability doesn't mean being perfect; it just means being honest and ready for the next time.

Celebrate others

This one's easy to forget when things are busy, but it makes a huge difference. I've seen how far a 'thank you' or a quiet 'well done' can go. People want to feel valued, and it's our job as leaders to make sure they do. Thank people publicly but also privately; there is a difference, and both are important.

Focus on solutions

It's easy to get stuck in what's going wrong. If I focused on what was going wrong, I would never have achieved anything. But I've learned that leaders are the ones who say, 'Alright, what's next?' Even in the middle of a mess, just shifting the focus to what we can do is powerful. The mantra to keep moving directly supports finding a solution or producing an outcome.

Inspire trust

I think trust is the real currency of leadership. You build it by showing up, following through and being straight with people. Once you've got it, you can achieve just about anything with a team. Trust allows other to lead, which gives permission to others to own their own story too.

Communicate clearly

I'll admit, I've never seen myself as the world's best speaker or writer, but I've learned that communication isn't about fancy words; it's about being real. Say what you mean. Listen properly. Be open, speak from the heart. That goes a long way.

I didn't learn these things in a textbook, though I am sure they all show up there. I learned them through my own lived experience, by making mistakes, being thrown into leadership roles and trying to do the right thing. I'm still learning, but these lessons have helped me lead through tough times, build strong teams and stay true to myself.

Surf lifesaving has been a constant thread running through the fabric of my adult life. More than a sport. More than a service. It's been a community, a discipline and, at times, a sanctuary. It has given me friendships that have endured decades, a sense of belonging that's hard to describe, and moments of joy and challenge that have shaped who I am.

I still remember the day I earned my Bronze Medallion in 2001 at Alexandra Headland. The sun was out, the surf unpredictable and my nerves were jangling. I was good enough in the surf, but not the fastest swimmer or the fittest on the beach. That small circular medallion, when it was finally presented to me, represented more than just competence in the water; it was an initiation into something bigger. I didn't realise then how far it would take me.

A few years later, in 2009, I joined Mooloolaba Surf Life Saving Club. From the very first patrol, I felt at home. Mooloolaba wasn't just a club; it was a family. Over time, my red and yellow cap became as much a part of me as the salt in my skin. I patrolled the beach as a member and later as a patrol captain, watching the sunrise from the tower and feeling that pride that comes from serving others.

As the years passed, I took on more responsibility in the roles of age manager, chair of junior activities, vice president and, eventually, president. Each role brought its own rhythm: the early mornings, the meetings, the tough calls and the moments of pure satisfaction when everything came together. Leading through the club's centenary celebrations remains one of the proudest moments of my life. Standing on that sand,

Age Manager with the Under 14's at Mooloolaba

surrounded by generations of lifesavers, it felt like the past and present were shaking hands.

During my presidency, we also achieved something long overdue – the final repayment of the club's debt. It had been hanging over us for years, a weight in every meeting. When the last payment was made, it felt like we could finally breathe again. It wasn't just a financial milestone; it was symbolic of renewal, proof that collective effort can restore stability and pride.

In 2024, at the Annual General Meeting, my time as president came to an end. I was voted out, a moment that hit me harder than I expected. Fifteen years of leadership, countless hours of service, and in one morning, it was over. Disappointed? Absolutely. But I've always believed leadership means knowing when to step aside with grace. The club was stronger, healthier and more united than when I began. That was more than enough.

These days, I'm back to where I started, just a clubbie again, training, competing as a masters athlete and patrolling with my mates. In 2025, I was humbled to receive the National Service Medal for my years of contribution. That small medal carried enormous weight, a recognition shared by so many volunteers who give their time and heart to keep others safe. Surf lifesaving taught me how to stay calm under pressure, how to lead without ego and how to give back without expectation. And, in return, my life experiences have made me a better lifesaver.

One of the greatest chapters came in 2024 on the Gold Coast, when I was part of the Mooloolaba Masters Beach Relay team that won a world championship. Craig Parker, Greg Toman and I stood shoulder to shoulder on the beach at Kurrawa, mates who'd trained, laughed and sweated together for years. The race itself lasted mere seconds, but it felt like time stood still. Every baton change clicked, every run was clean. We had practiced our baton changes many times in the months leading up to the race. When we crossed the line, gold was ours.

World Champions – Craig Parker, Greg Toman and Matthew

It was my first gold medal at a major event. I'd come close before, a bronze at a previous world championship, a handful of silvers and bronzes at the Aussies, but this one was different. This was a world title. On home sand. With mates who shared the same fire and passion to win.

I probably talk about that race too often, I know I do, but it meant more than words can say. It wasn't just a win; it was a reminder that perseverance always pays off. That age doesn't dull the edge; it sharpens your gratitude. That when you keep moving, no matter what, life has a way of rewarding you.

In 2018, I had the honour of carrying the Queen's Baton as part of the Commonwealth Games Baton Relay in the lead-up to the Gold Coast games. My leg of the relay took place on a sunny afternoon in Tewantin, on the way to Noosa, a stretch of road close to home. It was a special moment made even more meaningful by the presence of my family and a bunch of excited kids from our surf club's nippers' program, many of whom I had helped train over the years.

I was nominated by a nipper parent and friend from the surf club in recognition of my community work, and to be chosen felt both humbling and surreal. I didn't do the things I did for acknowledgement. I did them because it's what you do when you care about your community, but being selected to carry the baton was a moment I'll always treasure. And as someone who is genuinely interested in and follows all sport, this was made more special for me.

There was a genuine buzz in the air, cheers from the crowd, high fives from the kids, and plenty of laughter and photos. For a few minutes, I wasn't just a participant in the relay; I was part of something much bigger, something that brought people together in pride and celebration. It was a reminder that showing up, giving back and being part of your community matters. Carrying that baton wasn't just about sport; it was about spirit and a reminder of my contribution to the community. A short moment in

Baton relay with fellow relay runner Andy Fermo

time, but a highlight in my life. It was also a moment I would have loved to share with my parents, but I got up and enjoyed the time nonetheless.

That moment with the baton relay reminded me of one of Dad's bits of advice, offered in his usual thoughtful way at his sixtieth birthday – to make sure you have a work-life balance. It stuck with me. But like a lot of good advice, it took on a whole new meaning after we lost Mum and Dad. It's easy to say, but you have a whole new perspective on life and what matters and, perhaps more importantly, what doesn't matter.

Grief has a way of sharpening what matters. You learn very quickly that you don't get the time back. There are no replays. No rewinds. And while that lesson sounds like something you'd see printed on a fridge magnet, when you've lived it, truly lived it, you understand the weight of it. You start to see every day differently. Or at least, you try to. The challenge is how to adjust to truly live life.

But here's the thing: for most people, work-life balance will never be a balance. If you're anything like me, you'll always end up working more than you want to. It's not because you're obsessed with work or climbing the ladder, it's because life costs money, and work is how most of us keep the lights on. We live in a money society and sometimes you need money to do the 'balance' part of work-life balance. You don't need to be rich, but you do need enough, and for most people, that means showing up for work, often more than you'd like.

The trick, I've learned, is to fit the rest of your life in around the edges. Take the time when you can to find the joy in all that you do. To go to the school event even if it means logging back on later to take care of something urgent. To take the dog for a walk, to keep a Saturday afternoon that's just yours, even if Sunday is swallowed by the to-do list. It's waking up early and using that time for yourself. That's the real balance. It's not a perfect scale; it's shifting where you can to create balance, and the more you do, the more you will feel like you have some work-life balance.

What Dad was trying to say, I think, was this: 'Don't forget to live. Don't get so lost in the *doing* that you forget the *being*.' And if I've learned anything from the way he lived, and the way he left, it's that the people, the moments, the memories – those are the things that last. Dad died with few regrets, at least that is the impression I got. His life was pretty fulfilling, as he did the things he liked and loved. They were comfortable in their living and that will outstrip a bank balance every time.

I've learnt to become a better communicator, not perfect, not polished, but clearer, more honest and perhaps more passionate in my own way. Grief teaches you a lot about what matters, and one of those things is the importance of saying what needs to be said, even when it's hard. Resilience and tenacity aren't just about getting back up after life knocks you down; they're also about staying connected to people through it all. And that takes communication.

When you're navigating pain, pressure or setbacks, whether at work, volunteering or in life, how you talk to people matters. You learn to listen better. You learn that silence can be loud and sometimes what someone isn't saying is just as important. You also learn that people need clarity, not confusion, especially during tough times. That's where communication becomes part of resilience. It's what keeps the team moving, the family strong, the decisions steady. Sometimes I don't get it right, but often I do because I find myself speaking from the heart, not the head.

Sometimes, it means having hard conversations, or speaking up when you're tired, grieving or uncertain. But you do it anyway, because keeping people informed, heard and supported is part of what keeps everyone going.

I'm not the flashiest speaker or the slickest writer, but I've learnt to say what I mean and mean what I say. I speak with purpose now and I think people respond to that. Not because I always get it right, but because they know it's coming from a real place.

And finally, anyone can lead, you don't have to be the leader. Leadership isn't built in calm waters; it's forged in storms. When things go wrong, when people are afraid, when everything feels uncertain, that's when real leadership shows up.

The ocean that feels like home

The beach has always been my place of peace. The ocean carries a kind of freshness that never fades, a constant rhythm that clears the mind and, at times, Mother Nature's way of reminding you who is in charge. Even after years of living near it, I still get that same feeling of calm when I hear the waves or smell the salt in the air. There's something about it that makes you feel like you're on holiday, even when you're not. It brings me back to childhood summer holidays, sandy feet, long days in the sun and that pure, simple happiness that only ever seemed to happen by the sea.

Back in May 2013, our workplace had something called an 'ideas inbox'. Anyone could email a suggestion straight to the director-general's office. The ideas could be anything – small improvements, new ways of doing things or big-picture proposals. I was always one to have ideas floating around, and one day I sent in a thought that had been sitting with me for a while. What if we worked with the relevant agencies and community groups to establish Noosa as a National Surfing Reserve?

It seemed strange to me that Noosa, one of Australia's most iconic surf towns and point breaks, didn't already hold that status. I hit send and to be honest, didn't think much more of it.

Then, several months later in December that year, the idea came back to me with a question: could it be done?

The short answer was yes. So, I started the work, bringing together the right people who could navigate the approvals and make the case for Noosa's recognition. In 2014, Noosa was officially declared a National Surfing Reserve. Two years later, it became a World Surfing Reserve.

When I first sent that email, I had no idea what it would come to mean to me. It just felt like a good idea, the kind that fit the spirit of the place. I couldn't have imagined then how personal that connection would become.

I've always been drawn to the beach. It's where I feel most myself. I love the waves, the feeling of being in the water and walking along the sand. Surfing, body surfing, ski paddling and board paddling have all been a regular part of my life. Most days, I find myself near the ocean, one way or another.

I've never claimed to be more than an average surfer, and I tend to stay away from the crowds. For that reason, Noosa isn't usually my first choice, but it's also where I've caught some of the best waves of my life. Without a doubt, it's the break that's given me my finest rides.

And, as it turns out, Noosa was likely the first beach I ever visited.

It wasn't until July 2014, after Mum and Dad were killed, that I came to understand what Noosa truly meant to me.

In the weeks that followed, I found myself sorting through boxes of photos and old slides. Among them were a few that stopped me in my tracks: images of me as a baby with Mum and Dad at Noosa Beach. The dates on the slides read October and November 1975. I was seven or eight months old, on my first trip to the beach, and most likely my first swim in the ocean.

Matthew hanging with his dad at Noosa Main Beach in 1975

Swimming with his mum at Noosa Main Beach in 1975

In those photos, First Point looks almost the same as it does today. The scenery, the gentle curve of the bay, the headland and the golden sand have barely changed, despite forty years of development. The river mouth was different back then, further southeast near where the first groin is now. The southern channel dominated in those days.

Looking at those photos after their deaths, Noosa became something more than a surf town to me. It was a place that connected me back to them, to my first memories, my first swim, my first experience of the sea.

Even though the ocean had always been part of my life, I didn't own my first surfboard until I was fifteen. Prior to that it was boogie boards and inflatable surf mats. It was early 1991, and I was living with my family in Sydney. The board was a second hand, retro fibreglass twin fin from Kirra Surf – a 1980s classic, and it cost $99. I can still picture it. Yellowed from age, wax-stained and slightly battered, but to me it was perfect.

That January, I spent four weeks in Queensland, two at Maroochydore with a friend and his family, and two at Coolangatta with my own. I spent most of those weeks trying to surf, but I didn't catch much. I paddled hard, fell often and swallowed more seawater than I care to remember.

It wasn't until I was back in Sydney that I stood up on my first wave.

Manly Beach was the spot. Without a driver's licence, getting there from Castle Hill was a mission – bus to Parramatta, train into the city, ferry from Circular Quay, all while carrying a surfboard. It took around two hours, one way.

On one trip, a friend and I arrived at Town Hall station and walked up to street level, only to find ourselves surrounded by a massive crowd. Both sides of the street were packed with people. It wasn't the ideal place for two teenagers carrying surfboards, but a police officer spotted us, lifted the barrier and ushered us onto the road so we could make our way through.

Moments later, a motorcade swept by consisting of police cars, bikes and sleek black vehicles. We stood there with our boards as the Queen herself passed by, waving to the crowd and to us.

She was visiting Sydney to unveil a sculpture commemorating the founding of the city. I still laugh thinking about it: two young surfers, standing in the middle of the street with surfboards, being waved at by the Queen. It's hard to imagine anything like that happening now with today's security.

Looking back, it's strange how an idea sent to an inbox could end up meaning so much. Noosa's status as a World Surfing Reserve is more than recognition of its waves; it's recognition of its spirit, a place where natural beauty, surf culture and community all come together.

For me, it's also where my story with the ocean began. It's where I first felt the sand beneath my feet, where Mum and Dad held me in the shallows, and where, decades later, I found a connection back to them.

Whenever I stand at First Point now, watching the lines roll in, I feel that same peace I did as a child, the rhythm of the ocean, the sound of the shore, the endless horizon. Noosa will always be more than a beach to me. It's home, in the truest sense of the word.

Thanks just isn't enough

I will forever be thankful for many things. No one gets through life alone. Behind every step I've taken, every challenge I've faced and every small or large success, there's been someone in the background, supporting, guiding and sometimes just standing by.

This chapter is for those people.

The friends who showed up without being asked. The colleagues who backed me when things got tough. The mentors who challenged me to step up. The teammates, the surf club family, the fundraising crew and the countless others who gave their time, belief or kindness. Thank you.

Some helped for a moment, some for years, some without even knowing the impact they made.

What I've learnt along the way is that gratitude isn't just about saying thank you; it's about remembering, honouring and holding those people close in the story you tell about your life. In return, I try to be there for them; it's all part of helping others.

So, to those who walked with me, lifted me or gave me a nudge when I needed it, this chapter is my way of saying, I couldn't have done it without you.

At Mum and Dad's funeral, we took the opportunity to thank those who helped. The sudden loss is hard enough, but the task of recovering Mum and Dad's remains and bring them back to Australia seemed impossible. And if it were left to us with no help or support, then it probably would not have happened at all. I talked about this at the funeral. It repeats a little bit of our story, but I wanted to share a summarised version with you all.

On behalf of the family, I would like to thank you all for your love and support over the last two months. We are here today, a family in grief, friends and a community in mourning, before a world still in shock. We are all united not only in our desire to pay our respects to Mum and Dad but rather in our need to do so. For such was their extraordinary appeal that hundreds of people took part in their celebration of life just six weeks ago. Family and friends from all over the world lost someone close to them in the early hours of Friday morning, July 18, 2014, our time.

I want to share with you our story, or more so, Mum and Dad's story. You need to know that Mum and Dad have been in good hands. They have been cared for and looked after with the utmost respect. Furthermore, David, Adam and I have also been cared for and looked after.

The support for us during those first few weeks was amazing, if not overwhelming. Family and friends rallied around to make sure we were okay. Support for us, support for the kids and support for Mum's parents, Grandma and Grandpa. Simple gestures, such as food and meals, made those early days much more bearable, and we thank everyone for their contributions.

Six weeks ago, we could not imagine we would be here today. To be able to lay Mum and Dad to rest, together, in such a short timeframe seemed implausible.

How did we get here? When we learnt about Mum and Dad's fate, we had no idea where to begin. I suspect that this is a normal reaction when a loved one passes. But where do you begin? How do three brothers from different parts of the world bring their parents' home from war-torn Ukraine?

From the very first day, we had almost daily contact from the Department of Foreign Affairs and Trade. A consular official was appointed to us as our case worker. That person is here today. We cannot thank that person enough. It can't be easy to work with families in these situations, but for us to have someone to speak to and somewhere to go was invaluable.

The Australian Federal Police allocated two officers to our family. The AFP was also in constant contact. They helped us through the Disaster Victim Identification process and the DNA sampling that was needed.

We could not be here today without the help of these people and many others whom we have never met. Our thanks go to the Australian Government and the men and women who helped bring Mum and Dad home. We thank those on the ground who recovered bodies, people we will never know. We thank those who took them on the train from Torez to Kharkiv, often referred to as the 'train of death'.

Once in Kharkiv, under the care of the Dutch and Australian authorities, Mum and Dad were treated with the dignity and respect that they deserved. The days leading up to this point were traumatic and gruesome; however, it was the first step in the process to bring them home.

Dutch and Australian aircraft transported Mum and Dad from Kharkiv to Eindhoven. We thank those who flew them to the Netherlands.

On September 11, 2014, Mum and Dad arrived in Melbourne. Again, another special ceremony. This time we were joined by Julie, Rosie, Holly, Natalie, Heather, Glenn, Christopher and Carol to welcome Mum and Dad back to Australia.

And finally, on September 17, 2014, Mum and Dad arrived home in Brisbane, some two months after their scheduled arrival. They slipped through Brisbane Airport almost unnoticed. Almost as they would have done had they arrived on July 18, 2014.

Our thanks must also go to the funeral directors here in Brisbane. They have cared for Mum and Dad with the utmost respect since their arrival.

Of course, we are not the only family that faced this situation. On August 7, 2014, we attended the National Memorial Service in conjunction with the National Day of Mourning. It was on this day that we started to understand the scale of what happened. It wasn't just our parents or family that were impacted. Mum and Dad's passing was far from a normal situation. Our grief is shared with many other families throughout the world. We know that these other victims are also being looked after, and our thoughts are with them and their families always.

Our final thanks go to Mum and Dad. They prepared us for this occasion in more ways than one. Dad had ensured that their affairs were in order and instructions were left with us should anything happen. So, it was clear what we needed to do.

More importantly, our ability to deal with this situation and handle the outcomes is a true reflection of our upbringing and their parenting skills. Perhaps this is their greatest achievement. I feel proud to represent Mum and Dad, and proud to speak about them – to anyone who cares to listen. They have raised three good children, and I am sure that they are very proud of us, too.

We can't say goodbye without saying thank you. In their greatest moment of need, Mum and Dad were looked after. Indeed, we would not be here today without the help of many people, so on behalf of Mum and Dad and their respective families and friends, thank you for what you have done for us.

Epilogue:
Seeds of Hope

Before Mum and Dad passed away, I don't think I ever took much notice of the dreams that I was having. I have never really considered how they have impacted real life or the connection they may have to my world. I wouldn't regard myself as overly spiritual in that way. Prior to the downing, I had a recurring dream that involved a plane crash. The dream was always pretty much the same: large sections of damaged fuselage and me helping people who survived. I never saw the plane crash, but I was always first on the scene helping.

There were no specific location or any other identifiers. I never recognised anyone, and I generally woke up before any details were revealed. Sometimes I feel like it was a premonition, but there was no connection to family. Despite having the dream, I had no way of knowing it would happen to me. It was happening to others and I was there to help. What is weird about this dream is that I have never had the same dream since Mum and Dad died. Maybe it was a premonition, after all.

On the fundraising trip to China, I had spent a considerable amount of time raising money through my connection to Mum and Dad and what happened to them. It became something I was passionate about. On the first night in Beijing, I had a dream about my parents. It was so real. They came to see me to tell me what a great job I had done supporting the fundraising efforts. I felt like I was touching them; I was able to give them a hug and talk to them. I can't remember what we were saying, but at some point, we were crying. It was at that moment I woke up, my face was wet and I had tears streaming down my face. I was so disappointed when I woke up. It was just a dream, but it felt real. I am certain that Mum and Dad came to visit me in the dream.

You hear stories about people who have died and come back to life; they have had an out-of-body experience. There are numerous podcasts and shows about this sort of stuff. They recall that life is good and that people are happy because they are living only in their consciousness. They say energy never dies; it just changes form. I don't know if I believe in ghosts or heaven in the traditional sense, but I have a new perspective on energy. I'm sure I have felt it; some of these dreams feel real.

There are moments, fleeting ones, where I know Mum and Dad are with me, not in some imagined way, not just in memory, but in presence. I had never felt a presence like that before, but of course, I am in a different situation now. It might be a calm that settles over me when I'm struggling or a sign that my parents are with me. A flicker of intuition that feels like Mum's voice. I have found myself doing things that Mum and Dad would have done, but the presence through energy is different; it can be a bit spooky at first, but it becomes comforting. It could just be my parents' influence on me in my upbringing, but these moments feel real even though I know they are gone.

Sunflower in Ukraine at the crash site. Photo credit: Kate Geraty

Some people who have come back from near-death experiences say they felt peace. Maybe that's where they are and want to let me know they are okay. Maybe that's what I feel, not grief pulling me down, but a kind of peace holding me up. In many ways, it is like the sunflowers, providing a sense of hope and turning to each other when the sun isn't shining.

Ukraine is known for its sunflowers, and the world's largest crash site was mostly within these sunflower fields. Sunflowers are more than just a beautiful crop in Ukraine, they're a national symbol of peace and resilience, and one of the country's most important agricultural exports. Ukraine has long been one of the world's leading producers of sunflower oil, with the flower playing a vital role in the local economy and rural life.

One of the most moving gestures following the MH17 tragedy came from journalist Paul McGeough. Reporting from the vast sunflower fields of eastern Ukraine, the very landscape where much of the wreckage fell, Paul noticed the striking contrast between the beauty of the sunflowers and the devastation around them. Quietly, and with great care, he collected sunflower heads from the crash site, hoping to offer families something meaningful in the seeds, a symbol of remembrance rooted in the place their loved ones were lost. Paul wrote about his intentions in an article published in *The Sydney Morning Herald*, inviting families to contact him if they were interested in receiving some seeds. I wrote to Paul, showing my interest, and was looking forward to receiving some seeds.

However, prior to the seeds arriving in Australia, they were intercepted by quarantine authorities, a necessary precaution and in line with the strict Australian quarantine regulations. Rather than discard them, officials took the extraordinary step of growing the seeds in a secure laboratory, testing them for disease and ensuring they posed no risk to local agriculture. Only after they were cleared did the newly grown seeds reach the families of the victims. I excitedly received my packet, containing seventeen seeds. I prepared a garden patch at home where I could plant sunflower seeds, aiming to grow sunflowers and harvest my own seeds so the process could continue and endure.

Planting those first seventeen seeds, I hoped with anticipation that I would indeed grow some sunflowers, and I did. Most of the seeds germinated and grew into seedlings, with most growing into full sunflowers. It was not without incident. Insects and cockatoos seemed to like the sunflowers, but I managed to harvest several sunflower heads, dry them out in the shed and collect the seeds.

The new output was hundreds of seeds. I'd taken my seventeen seeds and given myself a real chance of continuing. I repeated the process every year, some years with different success, but nonetheless have been able to keep it going and it is very satisfying. I originally had no real plans for the seeds, other than to try and keep them going for myself. Then, I saw that with so many extras, there was an opportunity to share the hope with others.

One of the most meaningful connections I've made in recent years has been with endED, an eating disorder charity based on the Sunshine Coast. Founded by Mark and Gayle Forbes, endED was born from lived experience, from a place of deep compassion and a desire to help others find their way through one of life's most complex and misunderstood challenges.

What makes endED special isn't just its programs or its purpose, but its heart, built on lived experience. It's a community that listens, supports and walks alongside those living with or recovering from eating disorders, as well as their families. Being part of that journey, even in a small way, reminded me that healing can come in many forms: through connection, through empathy and through the simple act of showing up for others.

On July 13, 2021, I was invited to tell my story at the endED Espresso Bar as part of a speaker series they were running at the time. I'd not previously done that sort of speaking in the past, so this was a challenge just generally, but also emotionally. The flyer for promoting the presentation described it as 'An inspiring story of a Sunshine Coast local who turned adversity into opportunity' and that it was 'not to be missed'. I prepared a few notes, but wasn't sure how I would go, so I just went with it. I remember starting to speak and I just kept talking. I ended up speaking for about ninety minutes straight. I'm not sure how I did it. There was a small crowd of about twenty people who were captivated, listened to every word, cried at different times, but were clearly engaged and listening to what I was saying. I was emotionally drained at the end and was incredibly tired, but overall, I would say it was healing. The presentation must have gone well, as I was booked to do a paid speaking engagement with a local business at one of their conferences.

To close out my talk, I spoke about the sunflower seeds, how they made their way to Australia and how I had grown them and harvested the seeds to grow again. I talked about how they provided me with hope and shared this analogy: 'Even on cloudy days, sunflowers find their strength by turning to one another. Just like us, when the light is hard to find, we lean on each other.'

Following on from that presentation, Mark Forbes contacted me to see if we could use the seeds at the House of Hope in Woombye. The House of Hope is Australia's first residential treatment and recovery facility for people living with eating disorders. It provides a therapeutic environment for recovery in a tranquil hinterland setting. The facility offers holistic, person-centred care and represents a major step forward in how eating disorders are treated and understood in Australia.

It was an ideal connection, as these seeds don't produce ordinary flowers; they carry a powerful story. So, at Peaceful Park in the House of Hope, garden beds bloom with bright sunflowers every year. But these aren't ordinary flowers. Known as the Seeds of Hope from the fields of eastern Ukraine, they have become a living memorial and symbol of resilience.

I was honoured to be part of a special planting event with endED. I shared the story of these sunflowers and what they've come to represent. One of the lived experience team members at the House of Hope said it best: 'If there's no sun, they turn to each other.' That's exactly what endED stands for, too. Connection, compassion and community support during life's darkest moments.

A plaque has been placed beside the garden bed, telling this story, so that anyone who visits can take home a packet of seeds, and with it, a small but powerful piece of hope. Each packet of seeds is accompanied by the following message.

This envelope contains the Seeds of Hope, the fourth and fifth generation sunflower seeds that were harvested from the fields where the MH17 flight was gunned down in 2014 and brought to endED from one of Mark's close friends, Matt Horder.

Matt lost both of his parents on the MH17 flight and was provided with the first-generation seeds that were brought back to Australia from the sunflower field, where the crash site was in Ukraine. Since then, he has sown and harvested the seeds in his backyard and courageously shared his story with others. Matt was very warmed to be able to sow the seeds with us at House of Hope earlier this year and share the Seeds of Hope with people we support.

These Seeds of Hope hold the memory of all those who lost their lives on the MH17 flight and the hope of a better, safer tomorrow.

Now, the sunflowers stand tall as a beacon of that philosophy. The garden continues to grow and give back. When the time is right, seeds are harvested, packaged with this story and shared with others, spreading not just flowers, but comfort, strength and solidarity. They offer a small but meaningful reminder that even in grief, there is growth and in loss, there can still be hope.

In 2024, I joined the board of endED. I was drawn to the organisation's powerful mission and the real, tangible difference it makes in people's lives. Having witnessed the complexities of mental health firsthand, it feels meaningful to contribute to a cause so deeply aligned with empathy, care and long-term support. Being part of endED is not just about governance or strategy; it's about standing alongside people during their most vulnerable moments and helping shape a more understanding and responsive system of care.

One of the most powerful aspects of endED is its deep commitment to lived experience. The organisation is built around the voices of those who have walked the difficult path of eating disorders, individuals who know, firsthand, the pain, the setbacks and the courage it takes to recover. This grounding in lived experience gives endED a unique authenticity and relatability that many traditional services can't replicate.

It means people don't feel alone or misunderstood. They are met with empathy, not judgement, and they are supported by others who genuinely understand. And while my lived experience is different, I can bring a different perspective to support the organisation. Additionally, my experience in the not-for-profit sector and in executive leadership is sought after. Being part of an organisation that values lived experience so highly has not only been inspiring but also a reminder of the strength that comes from sharing our stories.

I knew my parents well. I knew how they lived, what they valued and the standards they held themselves to. The way they raised me didn't disappear with them. It's evident in my life, in how I work, how I lead and how I show up for others.

What I didn't fully understand at the time was the depth of what *they* carried. My father's steadiness, his sense of responsibility, the discipline he brought to everything he did. Those qualities make more sense to me now, not because they were hidden, but because I have grown into them. His work, his leadership, even his love of golf, were expressions of a man who believed in preparation, patience and doing things properly.

My mother's influence was different, but no less foundational. She was the emotional centre of our family, the steady presence that made everything possible. From her came my empathy, my instinct to listen before acting, my awareness of how decisions land on people. Where my father taught me how to carry responsibility, my mother taught me how to carry others. Together, they shaped the person I am today.

They never saw the version of me that emerged most clearly after they were gone. They didn't see the work, the leadership, or the life that unfolded in the years that followed. That absence is all part of the grief, which is something that is also shaping me.

There is one reminder I live with every day - my initials are MH. I see them constantly, on emails, documents, meeting papers. MH17 isn't just the name of a flight. It sits close to my own name, folded into daily life. Most days it doesn't stop me. But it is always there, a private overlap between who I am and what was lost.

MH17 didn't only take my parents. It took the conversations that were still ahead of us. The answers to the questions I would have asked. The stories I didn't yet know I needed. Time stopped, and everything unfinished stayed that way.

The day the sky fell, life split cleanly into before and after. There was no warning, no preparation, no sense of how to live in what followed. You just kept going, because stopping wasn't an option.

What I understand now is that while the sky did fall, the ground remained. It held the values my parents lived by. It held the lessons I didn't fully recognise at the time. And over years, not suddenly or neatly, it became the place I learned to stand.

I can't change what was lost that day. But I can choose what carries forward. In how I lead. In how I serve. In how I try to be worthy of the example set long before I knew I would need it.

The sky fell.

Nothing could stop that.

Everything after was choice.

Acknowledgements

For a long time, I could only imagine what it might be like to write a book. I often said I wanted to, but deep down, I didn't think I had the confidence or ability to actually get it done. Books always felt like something other people wrote; people with more time, more talent, or more courage. Even when I started, I didn't think I could get there. The only reason these words now exist on a page is because of those who have walked beside me. Each of you, in your own way, gave me a reason to keep going, and this book belongs as much to you as it does to me.

First and always, my mum and dad, Howard and Susan.

You gave me the foundation for everything. Your marriage in 1972, your move to Albany Creek, the house you built together – those choices shaped the life my brothers and I grew up in. Dad, I can still hear your voice as you worked around the house – and you always worked around the house, never sat still, really – and the way you'd offer advice when I was wrestling with a decision. Mum, I remember your gentle determination. You had a way of making sure things got done without ever raising your voice, and it always seemed so effortless. Losing you both changed me forever, but even now, your love and example continue to guide me every day.

To my brothers, David and Adam, we've shared so much more than just DNA. We've shared heavy silences, half-finished conversations and the kind of grief that doesn't always need words. I remember those early weeks when you stayed at our place on the Coast, the three of us sitting together, not knowing what to say but knowing we didn't need to. That was enough. We've stumbled, rarely argued, we've carried and supported each other, and I'm proud of the men you both are.

To Holly, you were the steady one when my world fell apart. I know that your world fell apart that day, too. You had enough patience to let someone unravel, knowing they'd eventually find their way back. You never complained. You kept life moving. You made sure Sophie and Josh had the routines they needed when everything else felt broken. You stayed when you didn't have to, and that is something I am grateful for.

To Sophie and Josh, you are the reason I can look ahead with hope. I know it hasn't been easy for you, growing up with the weight of what happened and the ripple it sent through all our lives. There have been moments that no child should have to face, and yet you have carried them with a strength and grace that makes me proud every single day.

Sophie, you've grown into someone with a deep sense of care and thoughtfulness, always noticing the small things that matter. Josh, you have a way of meeting life head-on, speaking your truth even when it's hard and showing a courage beyond your years.

It hasn't just been me teaching you; it's been you teaching me, too. Through your honesty and the ordinary chaos of our family life, you've reminded me of what really matters. This book is, in many ways, for you: so that you will always know our story, the hardships we faced and the strength we found in one another to keep moving forward.

To Roxanne McCarty-O'Kane and Leah Polwarth. You were the ones who planted the seed that maybe I could write this book. Attending

ACKNOWLEDGEMENTS

Leah's book launch really got me motivated to write my story, and Roxy, you gave me the guidance I needed when I doubted myself the most. Without that nudge, these pages might never have existed.

To Tony Abbott. When the unimaginable happened, you gave us leadership. You showed us that even as Prime Minister, you were willing to stop, listen and treat us not as headlines but as people. I'll never forget you leaning in during one of our first phone calls and saying, 'Tell me what you need.' It wasn't about politics; it was about people.

To Julie Bishop. If Tony gave us leadership, you gave us diplomacy, compassion and care. Watching you negotiate outcomes on the world stage while still finding the time to sit with families like mine was extraordinary. You carried the polish of a stateswoman but balanced it with genuine humanity. I'll always remember that.

To the Australian Federal Police. You helped solve one of the most complex crimes in modern history. I remember walking into that hangar and seeing the reconstructed wreckage, piece by piece, each fragment telling a part of the story you worked so hard to uncover. It wasn't just an investigation; it was an act of humanity. You carried families like mine through the darkest of times with compassion, patience and strength. To those who stood alongside us, your tireless work, your empathy and your refusal to let us feel forgotten will never be lost on me.

To the Department of Foreign Affairs and Trade and to those who walked beside us through the long and complicated maze of bureaucracy and diplomacy, thank you. You could have chosen to be officials, but instead, you chose to be people who cared. You showed empathy when it mattered most and gave a human face to a government response. For that, and for the countless unseen moments of support, I am deeply grateful.

To all of you, thank you. This book is more than just my story. It's a testament to the way people carry one another, often without even realising it.

About the author

Matthew Horder

Matthew Horder is a Queensland-based author, trusted manager and administrator, community leader and advocate whose life has been shaped by both deep personal loss and an unwavering commitment to public good.

With more than two decades of experience in senior leadership positions, Matthew has played a key role in delivering major community and sport infrastructure projects, ensuring the long-term realisation of benefits for the people of Queensland. He holds a degree in leisure management and a diploma in project management, and is known for his integrity, empathy and ability to lead complex teams through high-pressure environments.

Matthew's life changed forever when his parents, Howard and Susan Horder, were tragically killed aboard Flight MH17 in July 2014. In the years that followed, Matthew became a determined voice for his parents in justice and accountability, representing his family through the international criminal investigation and prosecution led by the Dutch authorities. His powerful victim impact statement, presented during the MH17 trial, was described by many as dignified, heartfelt and courageous.

Beyond his professional work, Matthew is deeply involved in community life. He has served in various roles across fifteen years at the Mooloolaba Surf Life Saving Club, including president, vice president, junior activities chair, age manager and patrol captain and continues to support fundraising and remembrance events. His reflections on leadership grief, resilience, justice and family have offered comfort and insight to others experiencing profound loss.

This memoir is Matthew's first published work, a personal record of trauma, love, justice and healing. It honours his parents' lives, reflects on the legacy of MH17 and shines a light on what it truly means to carry on in the face of unthinkable loss.

Book Matthew to speak at your next event

Add a bit of lived experience to your next event and get Matthew Horder – author of *The Day the Sky Fell* – to deliver a customised keynote to your team.

A corporate presentation from Matthew includes:

- A 30-, 45- or 60-minute keynote presentation.
- Question and answer session tailored to the theme of the event, taken from the audience, emcee or panel.
- Book signing with an author meet and greet and photo opportunities.

Copies of *The Day the Sky Fell* can be included in the price.

Example flagship keynote topic

Turning life's toughest moments into lasting impact

Your greatest challenges can become your greatest contribution.

We don't choose the hard moments; they choose us. What we do choose is how we respond and what we make of them. In this talk, Matthew shares how he transformed personal tragedy into purpose, and how the lessons learned in the darkest times can light the way for others. Drawing on lived experience, resilience and a belief in the power of human connection, Matthew invites audiences to see their challenges not as the end of their story, but as the beginning of their legacy.

Other example speaking topics

(Available as keynotes, breakout sessions or tailored workshops)

Truth hurts, but it heals –

How speaking your truth, especially the painful parts, can be a pathway to healing and connection.

You don't get over it, but you get through it –

Moving forward after loss with courage and authenticity.

Legacy: what we leave behind when we're not here –

Living with purpose today to shape tomorrow.

Leading through adversity –

How effective leaders remain steady, decisive, and human during crises or personal hardship.

The power of owning your story –

How telling your truth can inspire, connect and change lives.

From broken to brave: what MH17 taught me about humanity –
Lessons on leadership, compassion and persistence in the face of loss.

Beneath the surface: the stuff we don't talk about –
Breaking the silence around mental health and vulnerability.

The cost of carrying on: burnout, balance and being human –
Recognising the warning signs and finding the courage to rest.

Why your story could be someone else's lifeline –
Seeing the value in your experiences – good, bad and complicated.

When the system meets the personal –
What happens when personal tragedy collides with professional responsibility?

The strength of showing up –
The underestimated power of simply being there.

Legacy Leadership –
Leading in a way that influences beyond immediate results.

Head to www.matthewhorder.com.au

The website is the perfect place to buy Matthew's book, a Howard and Susan Pin and sunflower seeds in support of endED.

Testimonial

SEEDS OF HOPE

When, as a parent, you witness a broken medical system that is trying to support your broken child, the need to create change overwhelms.

My wife and I have devoted the last ten years of our lives to create that change. As a direct result Australia now has five live-in residential eating disorder facilities, a step-up, step-down, day program house, a short-term accommodation village and a community produce garden.

During this time we also opened an endED espresso bar, a public place where people could meet without judgement and share their own mental health journeys.

We invited community leaders to come to the café to share their stories and one of those leaders happened to be Matthew Horder.

Matthew expressed raw emotion as he relayed the feelings and mental anguish attached to saying goodbye to his parents in Brisbane, six weeks before they boarded flight MH17 in Amsterdam, and never seeing them again.

Sunflowers in front of the MH17 memorial in Amsterdam

The positive note that Matthew bought to his story was the promise of hope, particularly the Seeds of Hope.

Matthew and I then spoke at length about the Seeds of Hope and how we could ensure longevity and continue the story in honour of his parents and all those who had lost a loved one on the MH17 flight.

Our day program house, the House of Hope, was under redevelopment at that time and what better place to start the Seeds of Hope rollout then the House of Hope; a perfect fit.

Since then, we have grown many generations of sunflowers from the original seeds and have gifted a packet to participants who navigate our endED support services.

Matthew also tells his story at our annual fundraiser event where the audience then can purchase a packet of seeds to take home to plant.

Matthew now sits on our endED board and plays a vital role in continuing to spread our message of Community, Connection, Compassion.

Our community produce garden is approximately 2500 square meters and has over an eight-month period donated two tonnes of produce to Urban Angels, who in-turn deliver 15000 meals a month back to community.

The Seeds of Hope continually grow on this property and the garden bed is in the shape of a heart.

Recently the head chef from Make Peace Island visited our garden, was enthralled by the MH17 Seeds of Hope story and took some seeds back to the island for planting. Make Peace Island is an island in the shape of a heart and owned by Richard Branson.

Thanks to Matthew and his Seeds of Hope the MH17 story will live on for ever in honour of the 298 people who lost their lives, and particularly Matthew's parents.

THERE IS HOPE.

Mark Forbes
Founder endED

References

1. United Nations Security Council, Resolution 2166 (2014), United Nations website, 21 July 2014, https://www.securitycouncilreport.org/atf/cf/%7B65BFCF9B-6D27-4E9C-8CD3-CF6E4FF96FF9%7D/s_res_2166.pdf (accessed December 31, 2025).

2. Dutch Safety Board, MH17 Crash brochure (English PDF), Page 18, Dutch Safety Board website, October 2015, https://onderzoeksraad.nl/wp-content/uploads/2023/11/6a2c806849e0report_mh17_brochure_crash.pdf (accessed December 31, 2025).

3. European Court of Human Rights, Press Release issued by the Registrar of the Court, ECHR 173 (2025), 09.07.2025, https://hudoc.echr.coe.int/fre-press#{%22itemid%22:[%22003-8279845-11657965%22]} (accessed January 3, 2026).